Your Interests, My Interests

A visual guide to playing and hanging out for children on the autism spectrum

Joel Shaul

Jessica Kingsley Publishers
London and Philadelphia

by the same author

The ASD Feel Better Book
A Visual Guide to Help Brain and Body for Children on the Autism Spectrum
ISBN 978 1 78592 762 1
eISBN 978 1 78450 627 8

The ASD and Me Picture Book
A Visual Guide to Understanding Challenges and Strengths for Children on the Autism Spectrum
ISBN 978 1 78592 723 2
eISBN 978 1 78450 351 2

Our Brains Are Like Computers!
Exploring Social Skills and Social Cause and Effect with Children on the Autism Spectrum
ISBN 978 1 84905 716 5
eISBN 978 1 78450 208 9

The Green Zone Conversation Book
Finding Common Ground in Conversation for Children on the Autism Spectrum
ISBN 978 1 84905 759 2
eISBN 978 0 85700 946 3

The Conversation Train
A Visual Approach to Conversation for Children on the Autism Spectrum
ISBN 978 1 84905 986 2
eISBN 978 0 85700 900 5

First published in 2020
by Jessica Kingsley Publishers
73 Collier Street
London N1 9BE, UK
and
400 Market Street, Suite 400
Philadelphia, PA 19106, USA

www.jkp.com

Copyright © Joel Shaul 2020

All rights reserved. No part of this publication may be reproduced in any material form (including photocopying, storing in any medium by electronic means or transmitting) without the written permission of the copyright owner except in accordance with the provisions of the law or under terms of a licence issued in the UK by the Copyright Licensing Agency Ltd. www.cla.co.uk or in overseas territories by the relevant reproduction rights organisation, for details see www.ifrro.org. Applications for the copyright owner's written permission to reproduce any part of this publication should be addressed to the publisher.

Warning: The doing of an unauthorised act in relation to a copyright work may result in both a civil claim for damages and criminal prosecution.

All pages marked ★ may be photocopied for personal use with this program, but may not be reproduced for any other purposes without the permission of the publisher.

Library of Congress Cataloging in Publication Data
A CIP catalog record for this book is available from the Library of Congress

British Library Cataloguing in Publication Data
A CIP catalogue record for this book is available from the British Library

ISBN 978 1 78592 650 1
eISBN 978 1 78592 866 6

Printed and bound in China

PREFACE

We all devote much thought and effort into playing and hanging out. Children with autism spectrum disorders often find these less structured forms of social interaction to be very difficult.

That difficulty can take different forms. Many kids on the spectrum feel really good and comfortable doing their favorite things alone, so they do not explore options. Others feel quite drawn towards fellow students, friends and family members, but become overwhelmed with the complexity of other people's needs, intentions and perspectives, and thus choose not to bother with leisure interaction. This apathy and confusion places children at risk of retreating too far into their solitary activities. When that happens, children with autism miss out on many opportunities to enjoy their peers, family and friends.

Your Interests, My Interests is designed to help isolated and socially challenged children to develop motivation, knowledge and strategies for playing and hanging out. Children with constrained notions of play will find hundreds of ideas about what other people consider fun and how people can enjoy each other's company.

An earlier book, *The Green Zone Conversation Book*, explored common ground exclusively in the context of conversation. *Your Interests, My Interests* broadens that scope of common ground to include both words and actions.

Although children will enjoy exploring this picture-filled book on their own, it is also intended to be read with an adult. There are abundant opportunities to set up short role plays, and this kind of practice is strongly encouraged. Skipping ahead periodically to Part 8 is useful for this playful and productive kind of work.

This book is intended to be fun, but it is understood that children reading it may be experiencing lots of anxiety and discouragement in their social lives. Be prepared to devote adequate attention to Part 7, *When Hanging Out and Playing Is Hard*, to examine obstacles to enjoyable social interaction and look at possible solutions.

It is possible to use the book without the worksheets, games and other extension activities, but many children will learn better when this additional work is incorporated.

I hope that you, and the children you work with, find this book enjoyable and helpful.

Joel Shaul, LCSW

CONTENTS

Introduction — 7

Part 1 Jeff, the Dragons in His Head and the Kids at School — 13
Things to enjoy doing with other kids at school — 22
The talk together two-person worksheet — 25

Part 2 Sara and the Day that Keeps Changing — 26
The play together two-person worksheet — 34

Part 3 Ana, Her Screens and Her Family — 35
What do you love on screens? — 41
How much are screens eating your time? — 43
The family and relative interest app — 44
Plan how you might hang out and play with others — 45

Part 4 Rob and the Mystery of What His Family Likes — 46
Help Rob to join in activities with his family — 52
Practice talking with family and relatives — 53
Family members and what they like to do — 55
Things I can do with family and relatives — 56

Part 5 Jon and the Visitor   57
When someone comes over – things to do indoors   65
When someone comes over – things to do outdoors   66

Part 6 Alan and Growing Up So Fast   67
Help Alan to find more "big kid" activities   71
Help yourself. Do you need to learn more play activities that are better for older kids?   72

Part 7 When Hanging Out and Playing Is Hard   73
When playing is hard – a checklist   88
Hard things when someone comes over and things that can help   89
Hard things when I visit friends and things that can help   90

Part 8 Help 32 People to Play and Hang Out!   92

Part 9 More Activities, Games and Extension Activities   102
The play and hanging out challenge game   104
Words to ask, suggest or invite   108
Avoid leaving negative "memory files" in other people's minds   110
Leaving good "memory files" in other people's minds   111

INTRODUCTION

When you are all by yourself, you can mostly do what *you* want.

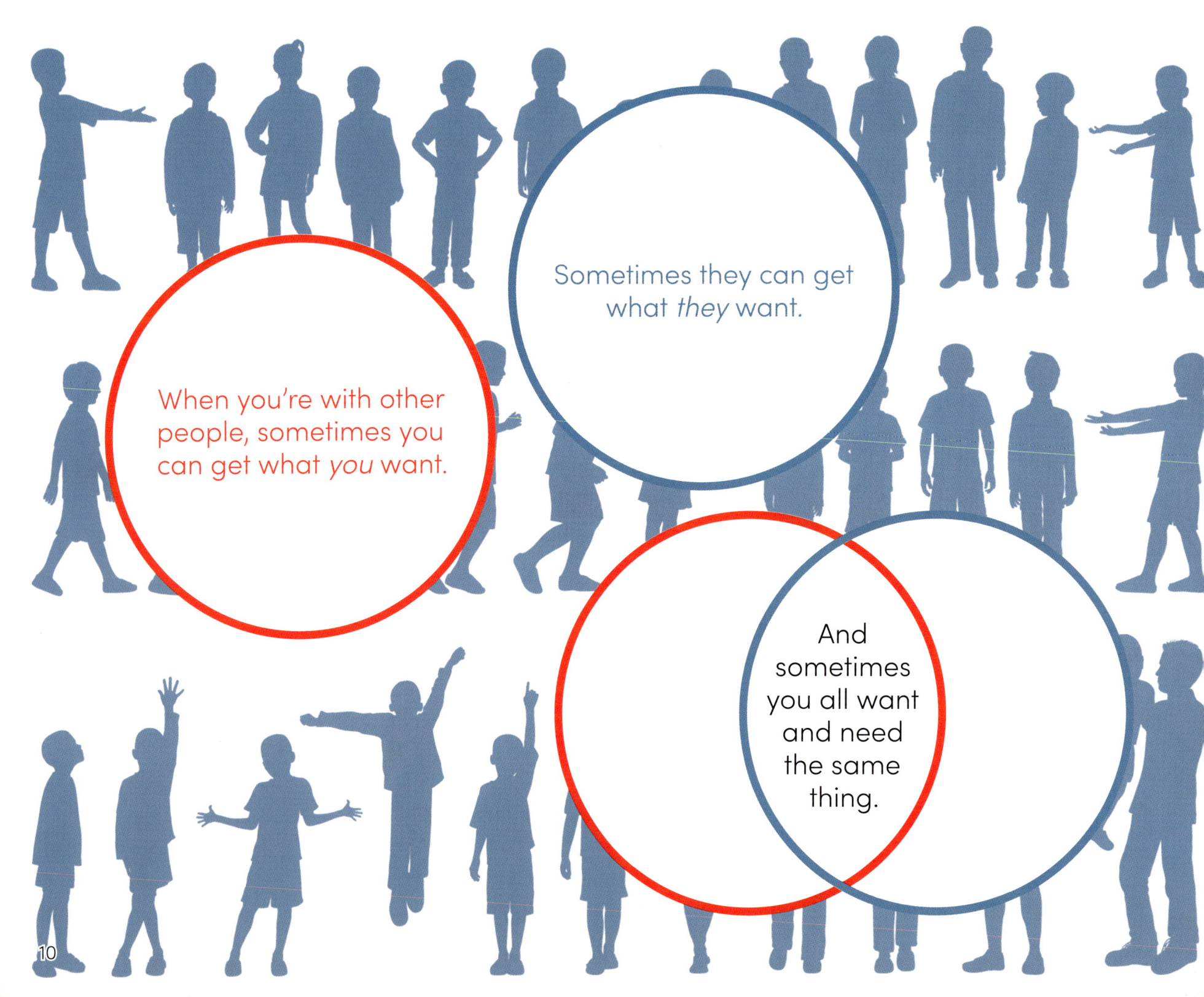

We can learn about what other people like.

That way, we can get better and better at playing and hanging out.

That's what this book is about.

Parts 1 through 6 are about young people trying to get better at hanging out and playing with others.

There are many activities for you in each part so that you, too, can learn lots of good ways to enjoy being with other people.

Part 1
Jeff, the dragons in his head and the kids at school

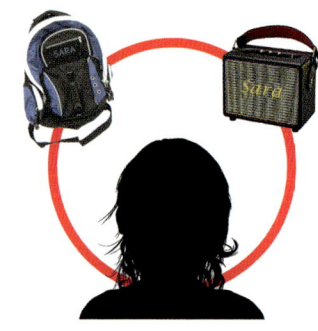

Part 2
Sara and the day that keeps changing

Part 3
Ana, her screens and her family

Part 4
Rob and the mystery of what his family likes

Part 5
Jon and the visitor

Part 6
Alan and growing up so fast

PART 1
JEFF, THE DRAGONS IN HIS HEAD AND THE KIDS AT SCHOOL

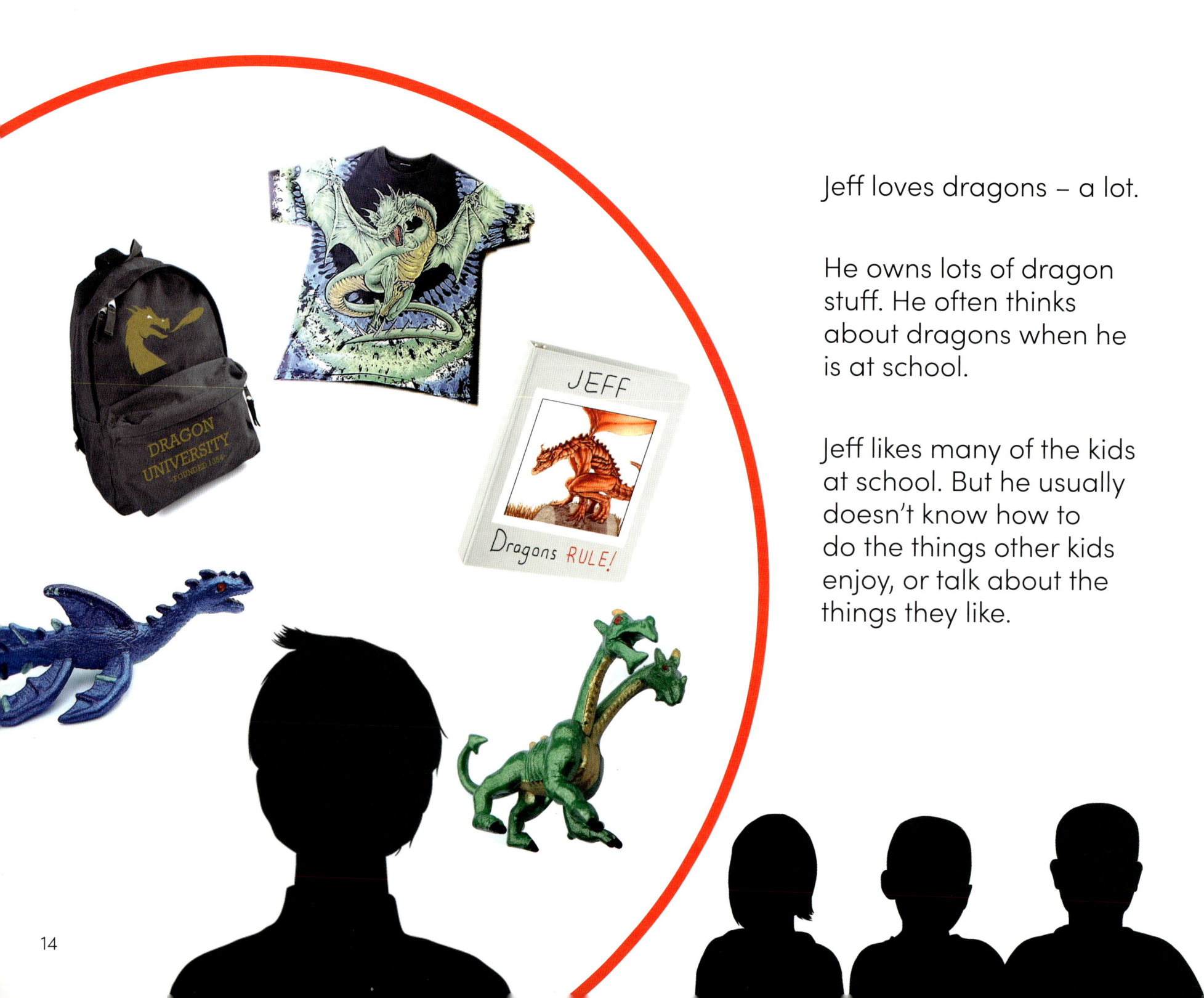

Jeff loves dragons – a lot.

He owns lots of dragon stuff. He often thinks about dragons when he is at school.

Jeff likes many of the kids at school. But he usually doesn't know how to do the things other kids enjoy, or talk about the things they like.

When Jeff is around other students, he often tries to make them do what he wants, and talk about what he likes.

Guys! Check out my new dragon stuff!
Do you want to play with my dragon cards?

He is so into dragons... Why can't he try some of the things that *we* like sometimes?

What Jeff likes

Some things these other students like

Jeff
- Website
- His sketchbook
- Cooking class
- Faraway places

Ava
- Helping to organize the classroom
- Cowboy boots
- Learning to draw things like fire

Cody
- Website
- Shows this to other students
- Pretty rocks

Vinh
- Wears this shirt (he is from Vietnam)
- He helps out at his family's restaurant
- Book he is reading

To get along better, they can take turns. So each person gets some of what they need, and Jeff learns about more fun things to do.

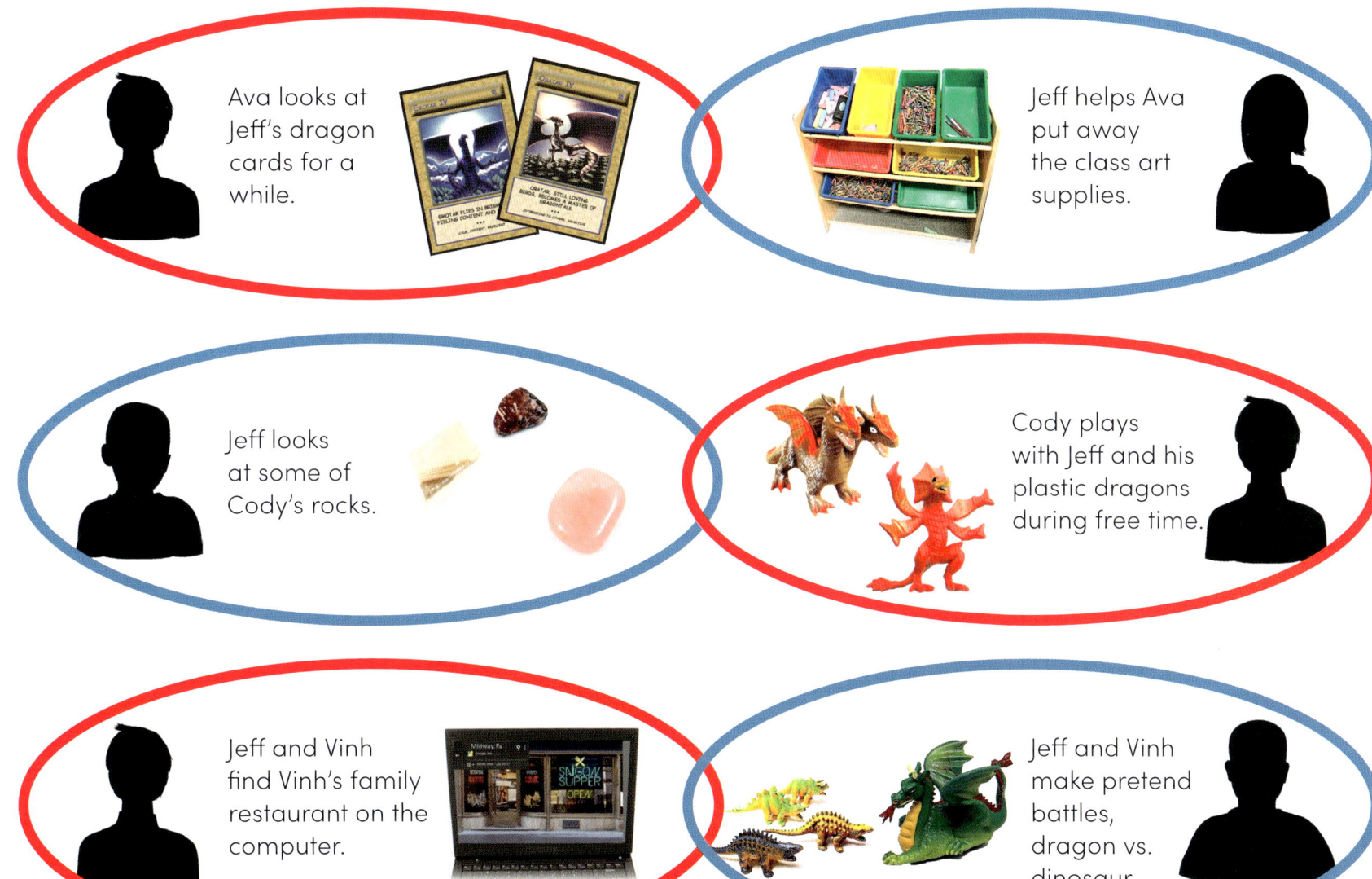

- Ava looks at Jeff's dragon cards for a while.
- Jeff helps Ava put away the class art supplies.
- Jeff looks at some of Cody's rocks.
- Cody plays with Jeff and his plastic dragons during free time.
- Jeff and Vinh find Vinh's family restaurant on the computer.
- Jeff and Vinh make pretend battles, dragon vs. dinosaur.

There are some things they can enjoy together. Jeff can find more things that other kids like. He can try doing some of these things.

He can get better at hanging out with other kids at school.

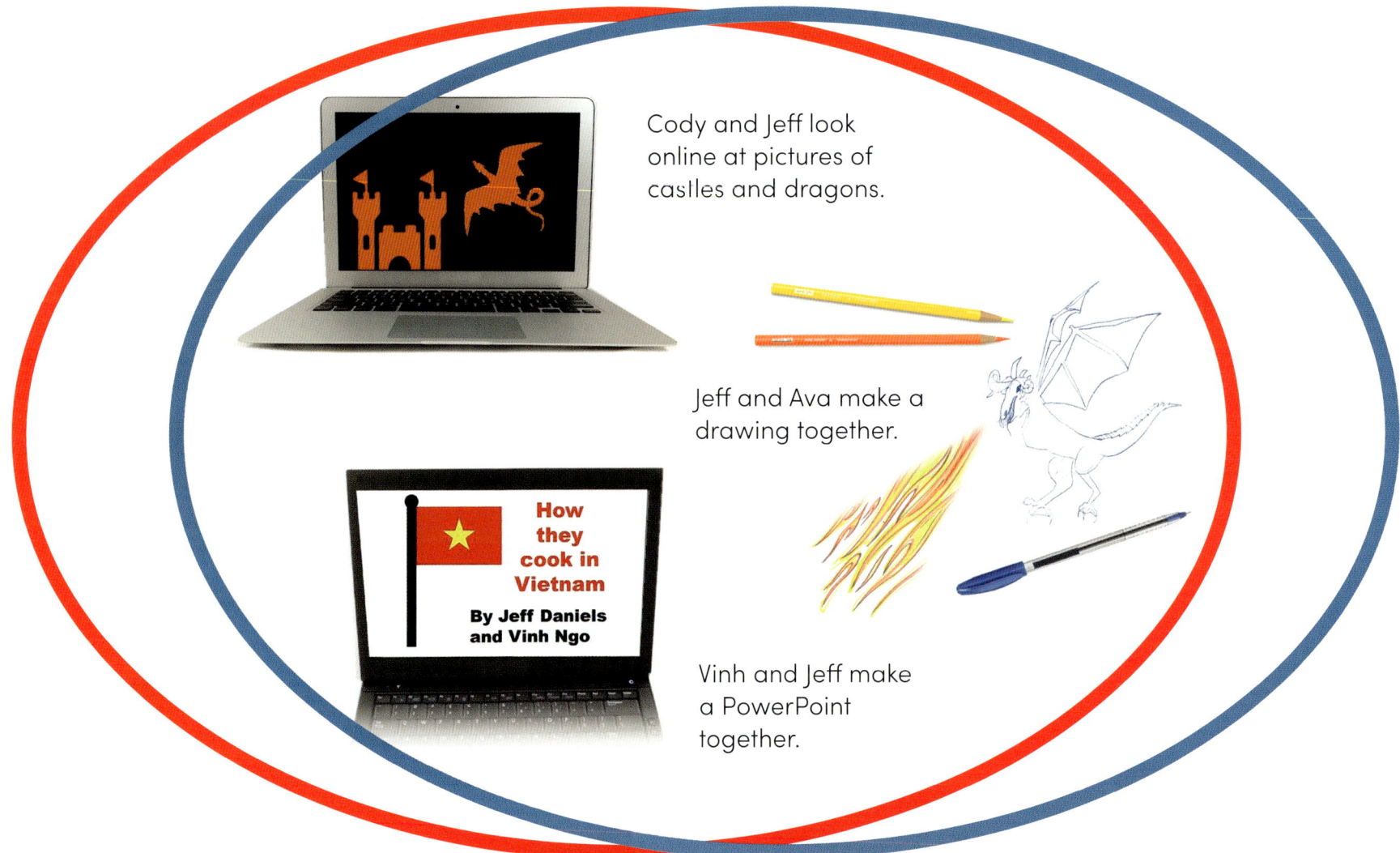

Doing things alone can be fine. But sometimes being alone gets to be a kind of habit that a person may wish to change.

Here are some typical things people do at school, both alone and together.

Which of these do you usually do alone?   Which ones do you usually do with other kids?

Are there any activities you do alone that you might like to try doing with other kids?

More by yourself...   More with others...

Looking at books alone in the library

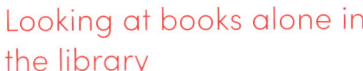

Walking between classes by yourself

Looking at books with other kids in the library

Walking with other students in the hallway

Eating in the lunchroom alone

Eating and talking with other kids in the lunchroom

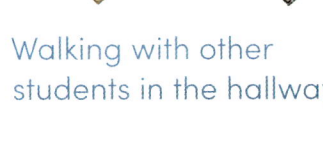

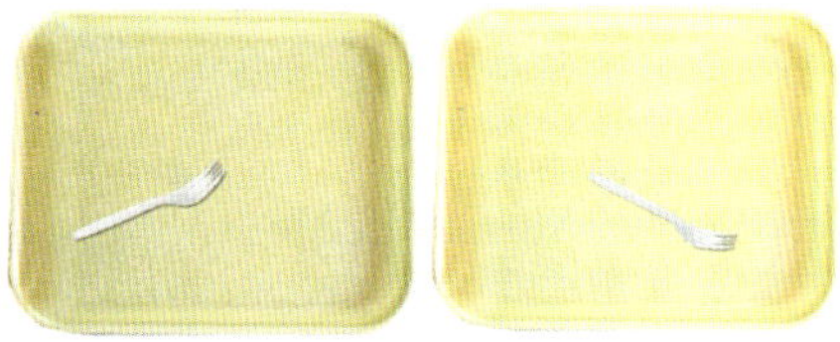

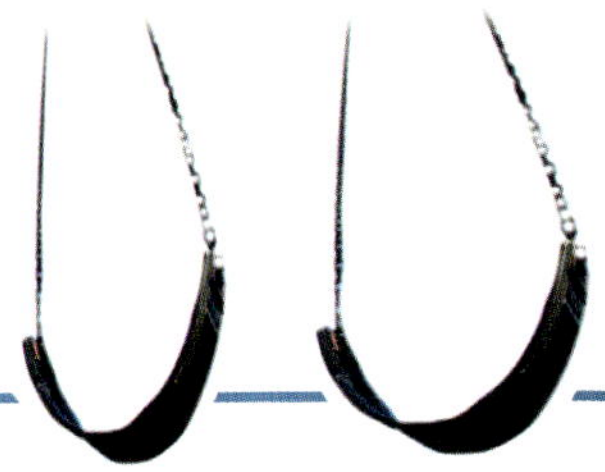

Enjoying the playground by yourself

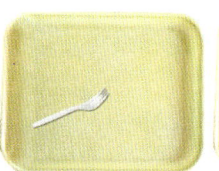

Enjoying the playground with other kids

19

INSIDE SCHOOL – THINGS KIDS CAN DO TOGETHER

There are so many choices. Be ready to try different things.

Work together

- Work together on an assignment
- Help someone with their work
- Let someone help you
- Notice someone's work and ask about it

Play together

- Try joining in someone else's playing
- Ask someone to play what you are playing
- Make music together

Find out what people like

- Look at what they seem to enjoy
- Ask about what they like
- Compare your hopes and dreams

Learn about each other's interests

- Help people learn about your interests
- Compare things about our life with the other person
- Explore each other's neighborhoods online

Eat together

Sit together

PLAYGROUND, SCHOOLYARD AND BUS – THINGS KIDS CAN DO TOGETHER

21

Things to enjoy doing with other kids at school

Playing by yourself is fine. But if you are thinking about hanging out and playing with other kids, it can be helpful to think up lots of ideas first. That way, if some ideas don't work out, you can try others.

In the six boxes below, draw pictures (or just write words) showing some things that you and other students might enjoy doing together.

HOW TO TALK WITH SOMEONE

Point yourself towards the other person	Think about the other person
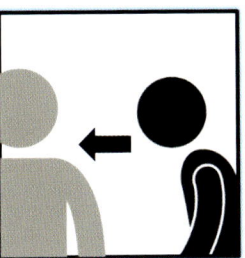	
Turn down other thoughts	Ask good questions
	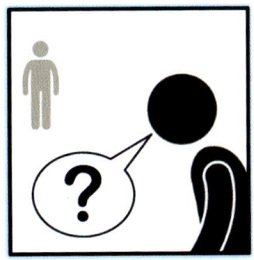
Talk back and forth	Be friendly and polite

THINGS TO TALK ABOUT

Things you both like	Things about the other person
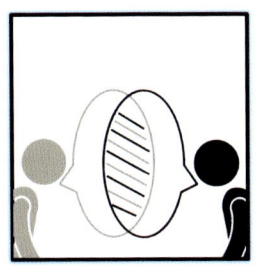	
Things about you	Happy things or troubling things

Things that have happened	Things that may happen

THE TALK TOGETHER TWO-PERSON WORKSHEET – TWO WAYS TO USE IT

First way

Two people, writing at the same time*, figure out what things they have in common – that is, what things they BOTH like talking about.

Second way

First, fill out the left side, writing down your own special things you like to talk about. Second, on the right side, write down what another person likes to talk about.

Third, fill out the middle part with the "matches" – the things that you both might enjoy talking about together.

*Adult: Position two children facing each other. Have them write simultaneously, not taking turns.

The talk together two-person worksheet

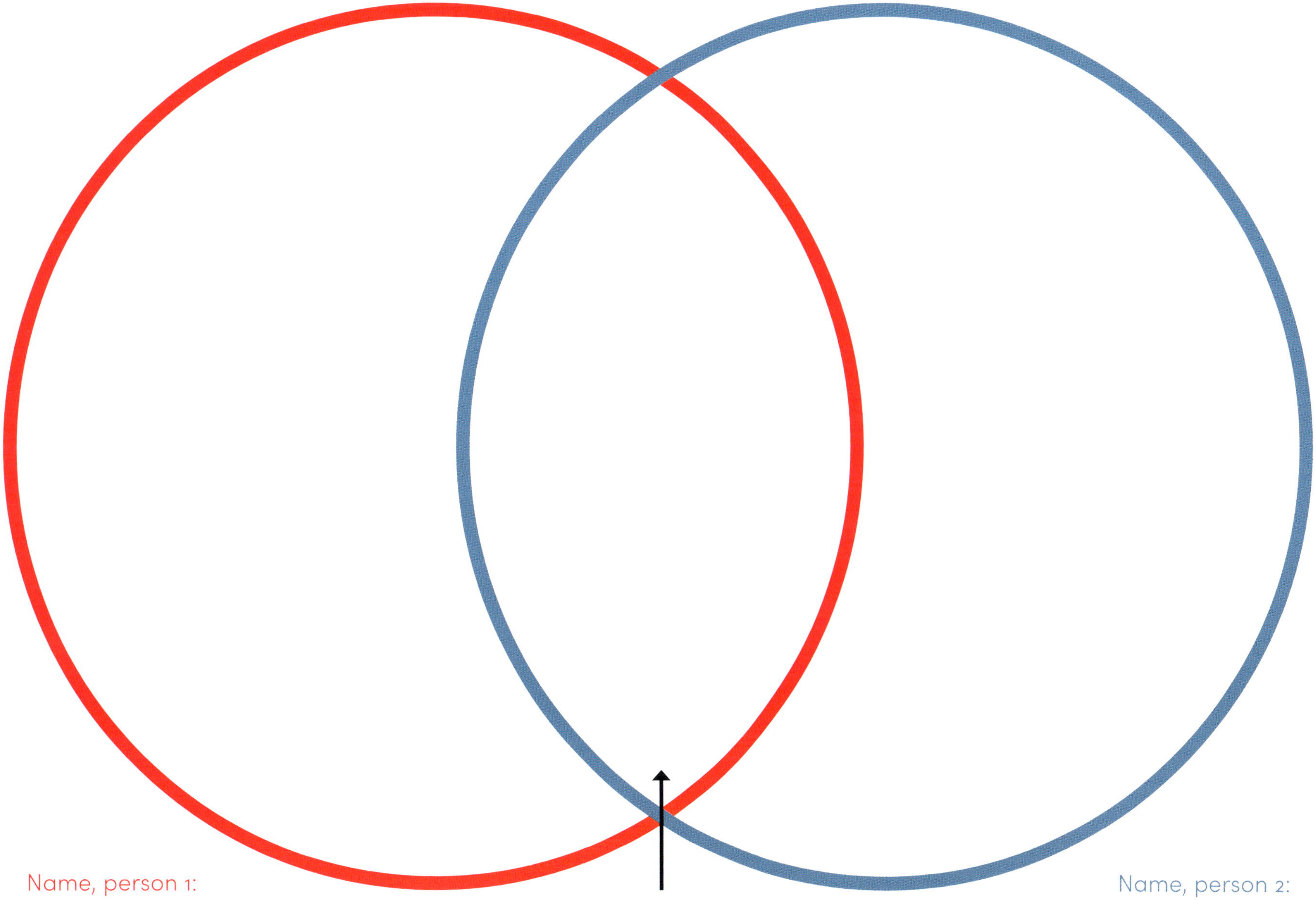

Name, person 1:
_____
Person 1 writes what he/she likes to talk about

Write down things **you both like to talk about**

Name, person 2:
_____
Person 1 writes what he/she likes to talk about

PART 2
SARA AND THE DAY THAT KEEPS CHANGING

Sara met Rachel at school recently, and they have started playing together at the Sunday School they both attend. Their mothers have been talking on the phone. Rachel's mom invited Sara to come over.

Sara is getting excited. In her backpack, Sara is putting everything she thinks she will need to have a really great day at Rachel's house.

Video game controller so she and Rachel can play games together. They have the same game system

Sara's phone so she can show Rachel all the things she likes

Sara's portable speaker to play the music she likes

Rachel

While Sara is making her plans, Rachel is having her own ideas about the day.

Playing video games with Sara

Asking Sara if she likes dolls

Finding out if Sara likes to draw or color

Taking turns picking out music to listen to

When Sara and her mom get to Rachel's home, Sara's mom and Rachel's mom go talk in the kitchen while Sara and Rachel start playing together in Rachel's room.

Sara starts to play her music.

Sara shows Rachel all her favorite things on her phone.

Rachel asks Sara if she would like to play a video game. Sara says "No, thank you" because Rachel does not have the video games she likes.

Sara is enjoying this play date.

While Sara is playing, the doorbell rings. Rachel's neighbor, Casey, walks in with dolls, magazines, pencils and hair stuff.

Rachel and Casey play and talk together.

Sara feels confused and left out.

She finds her mom and asks to go home.

Next Saturday, Sara gets invited to come over to Rachel's again. Sara thinks hard about the things Rachel likes – and Casey too, in case Casey shows up.

Sara asks for her mother's help when she decides what to bring in the backpack.

Sara feels hopeful. She is thinking about what activities she, Rachel and Casey all might like.

Hmm...I wonder what I should bring along in my backpack this time...

If I do bring my phone, I should leave it in my backpack. It distracts me and then I can't stop looking at it.

I should probably leave my speaker at home. Maybe I can ask Rachel if we all can take turns listening to songs on her own music player.

Sara has some better ideas now about how she might play at Rachel's house. She is thinking of things everyone might enjoy doing together.

Drawing might be nice to do together. Rachel and Casey seem to like drawing and they can pick different things to draw.

Listening to music might work out. Sara could ask if Rachel wants to play some music, and then they can all take turns picking songs.

Sara's mother has an idea. A Comic Convention that all three girls might like is coming to a nearby town.

Sara thinks about joining a Girl Scout Troop that Rachel and Casey belong to.

THE PLAY TOGETHER TWO-PERSON WORKSHEET – TWO WAYS TO USE IT

This is like the Talk Together Two-Person Worksheet (pages 24–25) but instead it's to help two people figure out what things they both like to play.

First way

Two people, writing at the same time*, figure out what play activities they both like.

Second way

You can also use this worksheet by yourself.

First, fill out the left side, writing down your own special things you like to do when you play.

Second, on the right side, write down what another person likes doing when they play.

Third, fill out the middle part with the "matches" – the things that you both might like doing together.

*Adult: Position two children facing each other. Have them write simultaneously, not taking turns.

33

The play together two-person worksheet

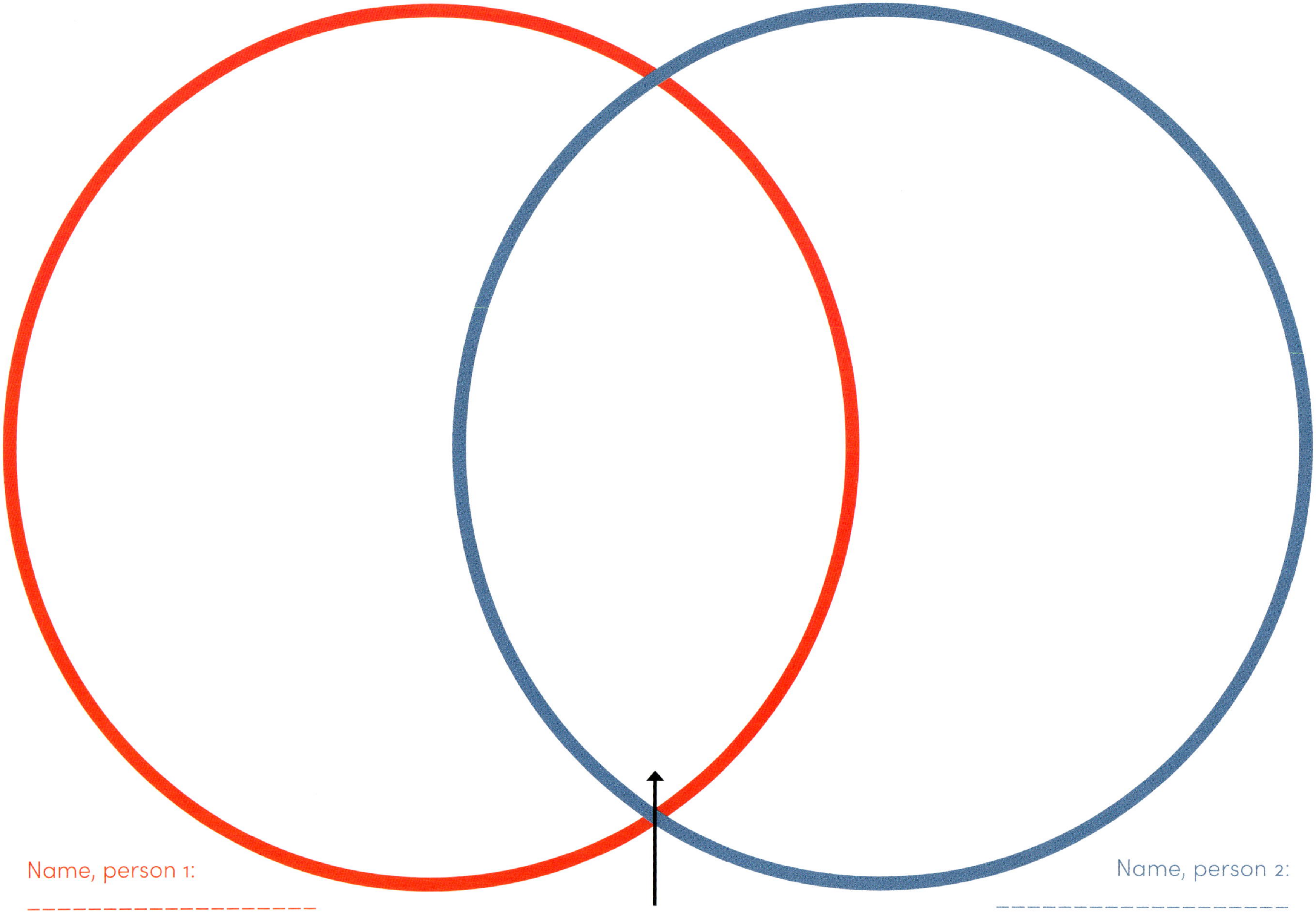

Name, person 1:
_____
Person 1 writes play and hanging out activities he/she likes

Write down playing and hanging out activities **you both like**

Name, person 2:
_____
Person 1 writes play and hanging out activities he/she likes

PART 3
ANA, HER SCREENS AND HER FAMILY

Ana's screens mean so much to her.

It was only normal for Ana to give up her little girl toys as she got older.

But then her interest in video games and game characters grew and grew – until she knew the games better than she knew people in her family.

Now, she feels strongly connected to her video game friends in multiplayer games.

On Ana's screens, the battles she fights and the things she creates feel very important. In some ways they feel more important than whatever Ana might do with her own family.

It feels sometimes like she loves her electronics more than she loves us.

What Ana likes

Ana
- Playing her favorite video games
- Watching video game videos
- Watching TV
- Eating homemade cookies

Some things Ana's family likes

Dad
- Baking things
- Good times with the family
- Relaxing and watching cooking shows
- Fishing

Step-mom
- Her construction job
- Nice shoes and clothes
- Working in the yard

Brother Dave
- Playing his favorite video games
- Outdoor play in the yard
- Playing with puppets

38

To get along better, they can take turns. So each person gets some of what they need, and Ana is not alone quite so much.

- Dave sits and watches video game videos with Ana for a while.

- Ana plays puppets with Dave for a while.

- Ana and her step-mom go out shopping first for clothes...

- ...and then for a video game for Ana.

- Ana helps Dad sort out his recipe box.

- Ana and Dad take turns watching each other's shows.

Ana can still spend time alone – just less. After she enjoys some alone time, she can enjoy many things together with her family.

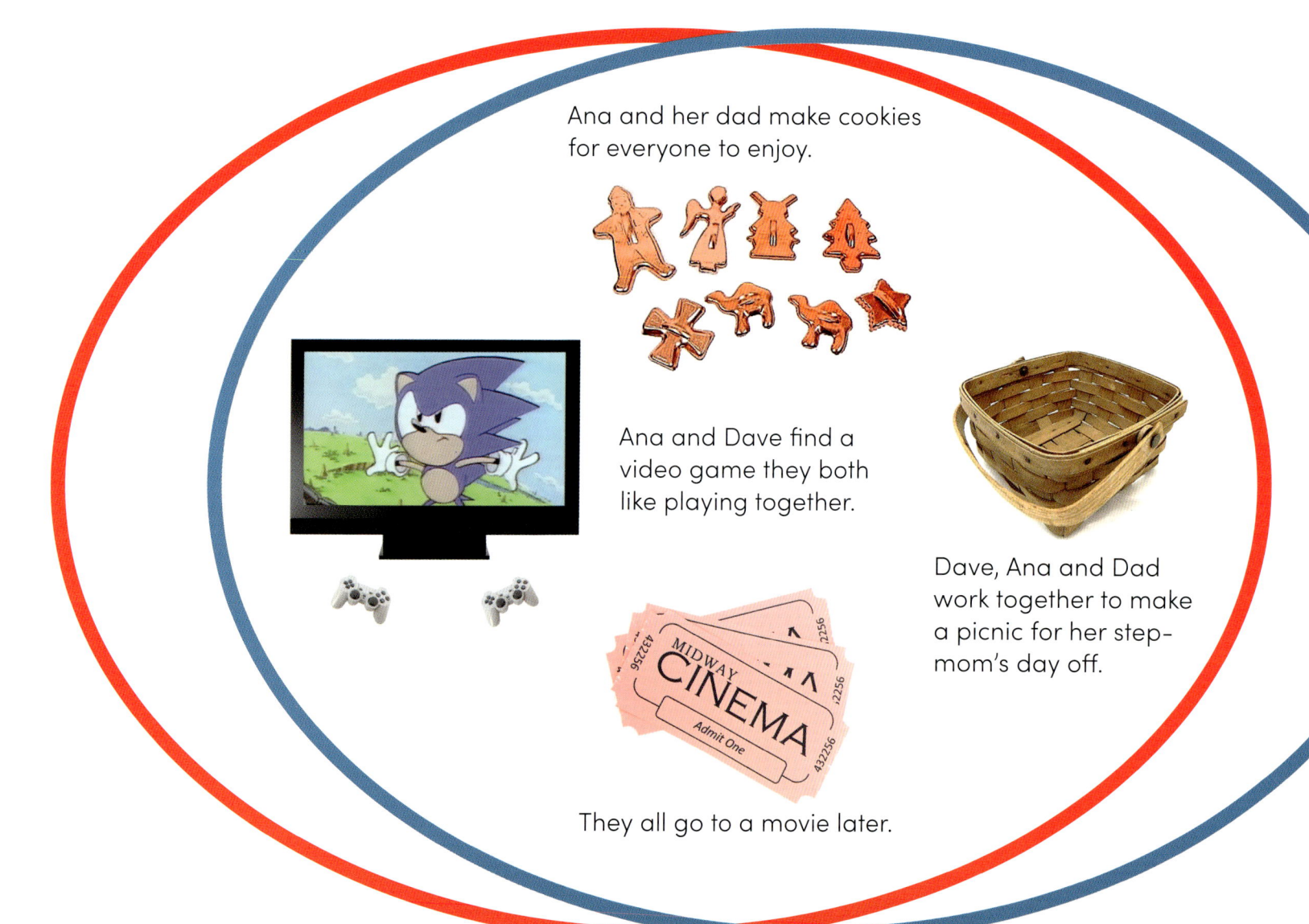

Ana and her dad make cookies for everyone to enjoy.

Ana and Dave find a video game they both like playing together.

Dave, Ana and Dad work together to make a picnic for her stepmom's day off.

They all go to a movie later.

What do you love on screens?

Lots of people love TV, video games, tablets, phones or computers. On the screens shown here, draw or write a few of your favorite screen activities.

Here is a chart Ana filled out showing what her days were usually like before she started to spend more time with her family.

How do you spend your own time when you are not in school?

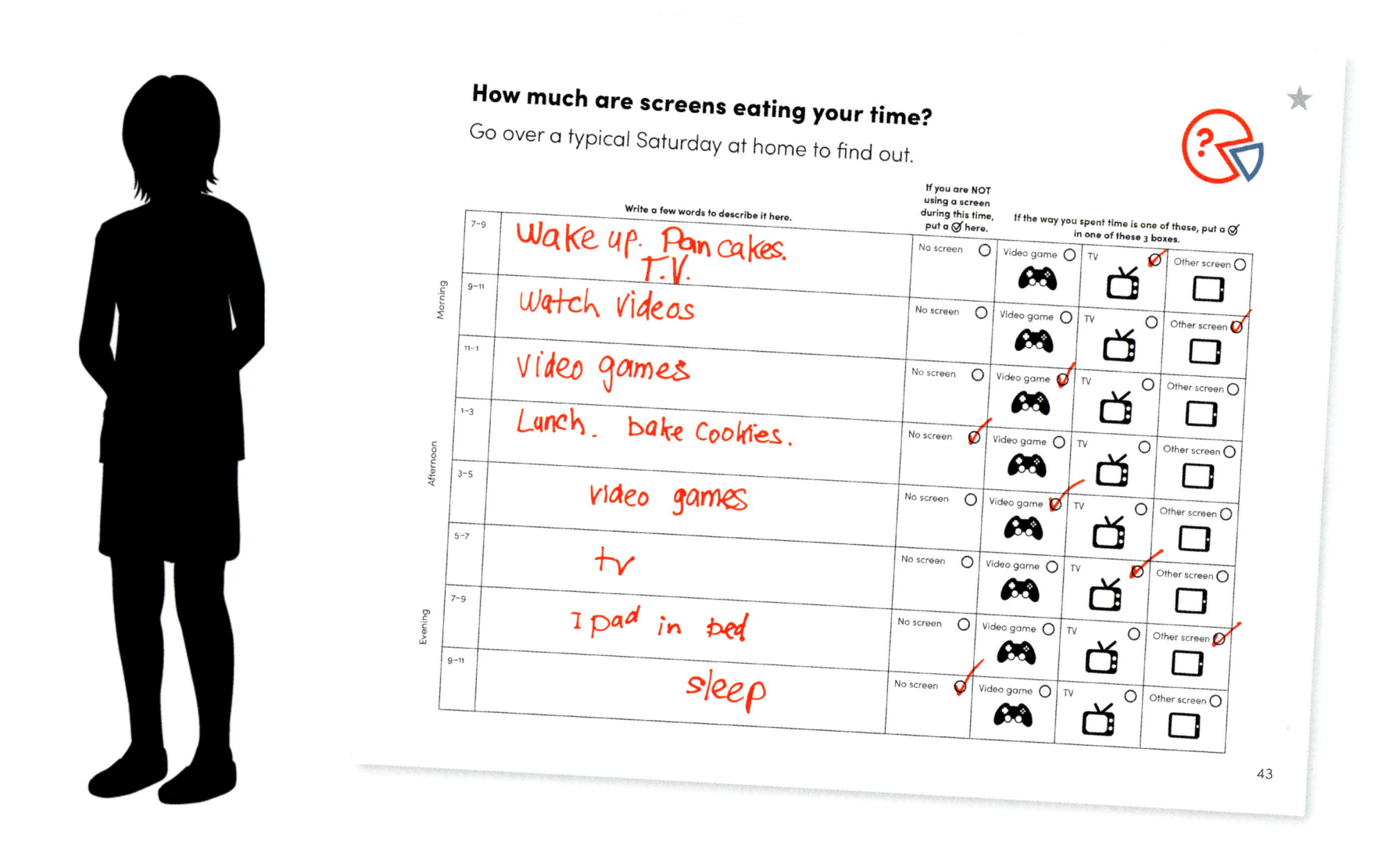

How much are screens eating your time?

Go over a typical Saturday at home to find out.

Time		Write a few words to describe it here.	If you are NOT using a screen during this time, put a ✓ here.	If the way you spent time is one of these, put a ✓ in one of these 3 boxes.		
				Video game	TV	Other screen
7–9	Morning	Wake up. Pancakes. T.V.	No screen	Video game	TV ✓	Other screen
9–11		watch videos	No screen	Video game	TV	Other screen ✓
11–1	Afternoon	video games	No screen	Video game ✓	TV	Other screen
1–3		Lunch. bake cookies.	No screen ✓	Video game	TV	Other screen
3–5		video games	No screen	Video game ✓	TV	Other screen
5–7	Evening	tv	No screen	Video game	TV ✓	Other screen
7–9		Ipad in bed	No screen	Video game	TV	Other screen ✓
9–11		sleep	No screen ✓	Video game	TV	Other screen

How much are screens eating *your* time?

Go over a typical Saturday at home to find out.

		Write a few words to describe it here.	If you are NOT using a screen during this time, put a ✓ here.	If the way you spent time is one of these, put a ✓ in one of these 3 boxes.		
Morning	7–9		No screen ○	Video game ○	TV ○	Other screen ○
	9–11		No screen ○	Video game ○	TV ○	Other screen ○
	11–1		No screen ○	Video game ○	TV ○	Other screen ○
Afternoon	1–3		No screen ○	Video game ○	TV ○	Other screen ○
	3–5		No screen ○	Video game ○	TV ○	Other screen ○
Evening	5–7		No screen ○	Video game ○	TV ○	Other screen ○
	7–9		No screen ○	Video game ○	TV ○	Other screen ○
	9–11		No screen ○	Video game ○	TV ○	Other screen ○

The family and relative interest app

Imagine if there was an app that would let you know what someone in your family enjoys doing!

Copy this page for one or more family members and relatives. On each sheet, fill in the blanks and draw pictures to show what is important to the person.

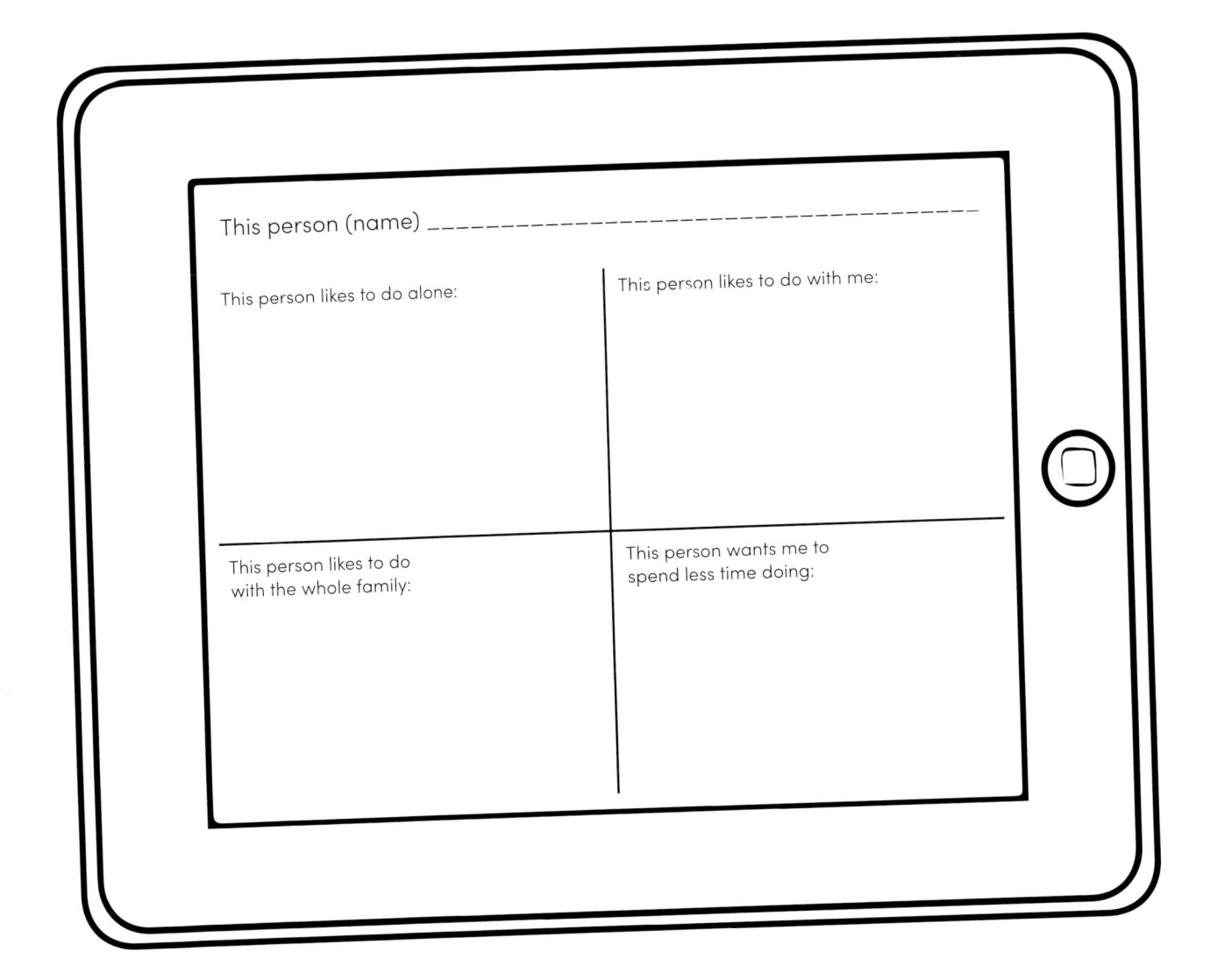

This person (name) _____

This person likes to do alone:

This person likes to do with me:

This person likes to do with the whole family:

This person wants me to spend less time doing:

Plan how you might hang out and play with others

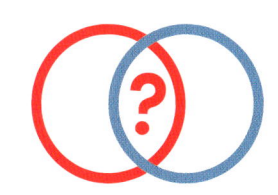

Imagine a Saturday sometime in the near future when you spend *less* time all alone. Describe what that day might be like.

Briefly describe this day you are planning in the blanks below.

Morning	7–9	
	9–11	
	11–1	
Afternoon	1–3	
	3–5	
	5–7	
Evening	7–9	
	9–11	

PART 4
ROB AND THE MYSTERY OF WHAT HIS FAMILY LIKES

Rob loves doing his favorite things – a lot.

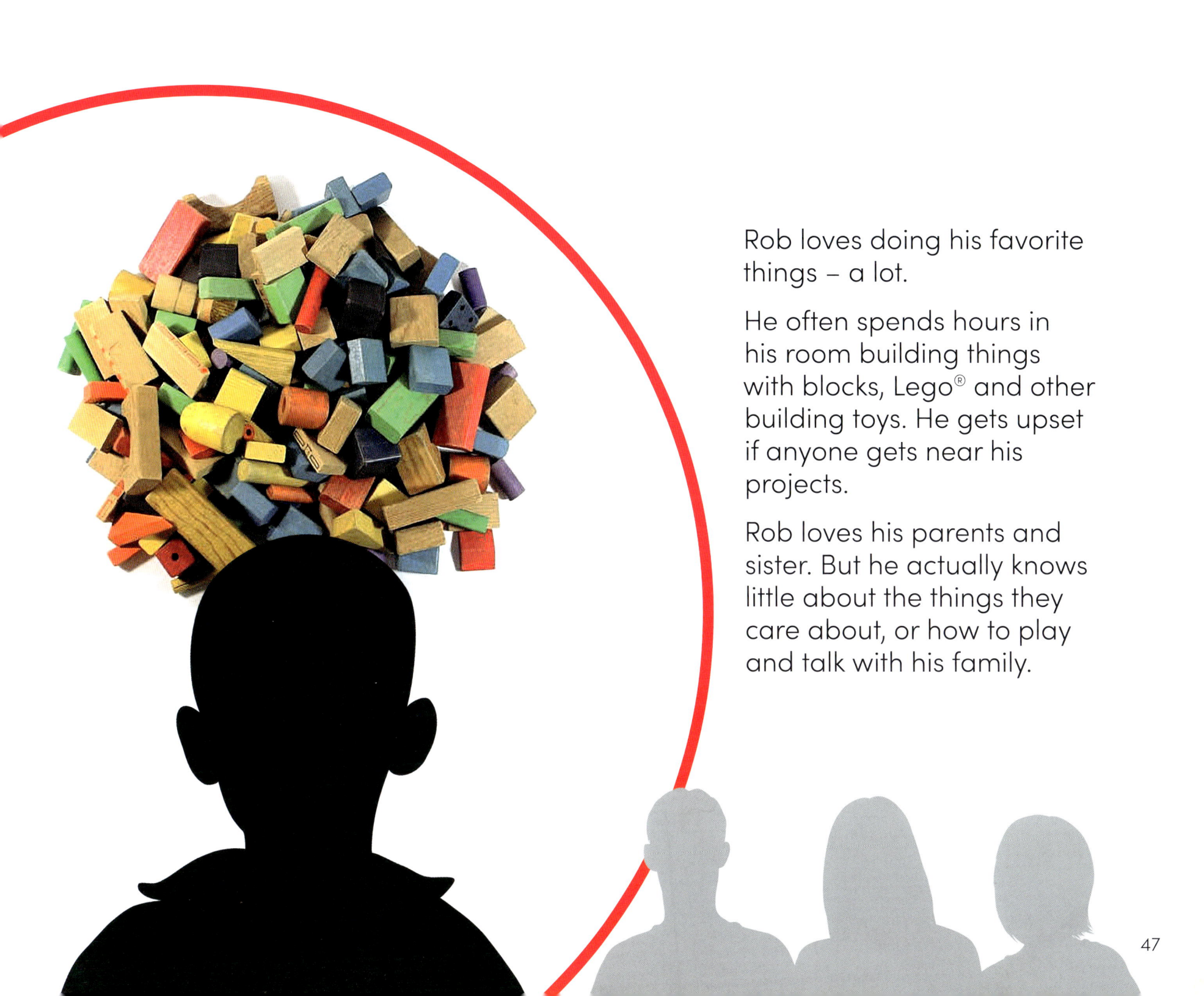

He often spends hours in his room building things with blocks, Lego® and other building toys. He gets upset if anyone gets near his projects.

Rob loves his parents and sister. But he actually knows little about the things they care about, or how to play and talk with his family.

When Rob does spend time with his family, he often ends up trying to get them to do things he likes.

Mom! Dad! Eva! You gotta see this video I found about Lego®!

It's nice to hang out with Rob... but do we always have to look at his Lego® videos?

What Rob likes

- Toys for building
- More toys for building
- Watching YouTube videos
- Learning how to paint

Rob

Some things Rob's family likes

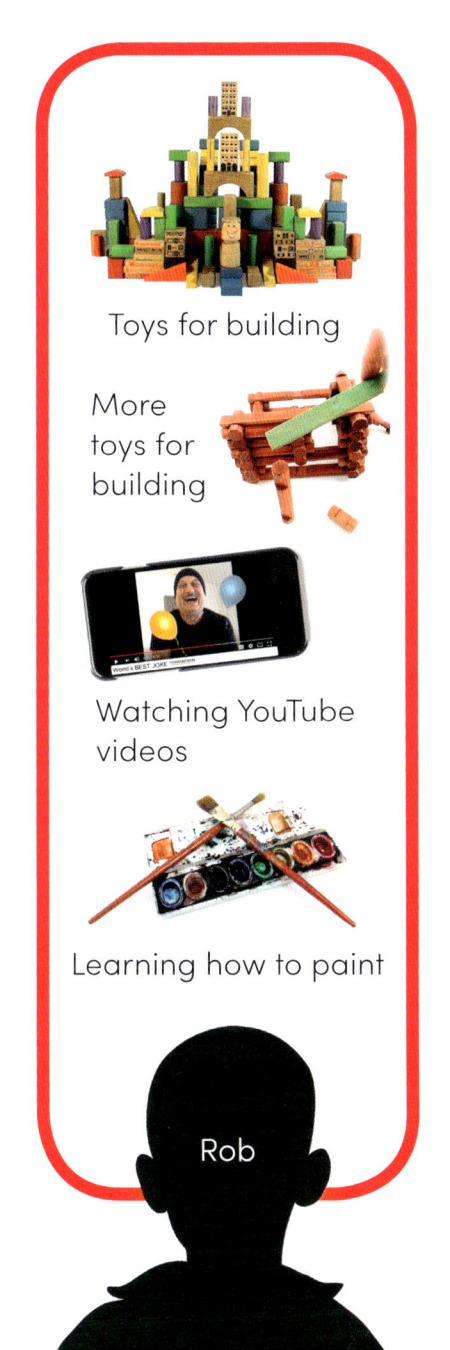

- Hiking with a backpack
- Home repair projects
- Taking videos and photos

Dad

- Collecting old alarm clocks
- African drumming
- Buying cat stuff for her shelves

Mum

- Trying to make their bird talk
- Hanging out with Rob
- Playing with action figures
- Drawing pictures

Eva

49

To get along better, they can take turns. So each person gets some of what they need, and Rob learns about more fun things to do.

- Rob plays with Eva's action figures for a while, even though he does not like them much.

- Eva looks at funny videos with Rob.

- Rob and his mom go to a shop where Rob can buy used Lego® stuff he wants.

- Rob's mom checks out some old cat figurines at that same shop.

- Rob learns how to use tools with his dad.

- Dad and Rob build something with Lego®.

There are lots of things they can enjoy together. Rob can find more things his family likes. He can try doing some of these things.

He can get better at hanging out with people.

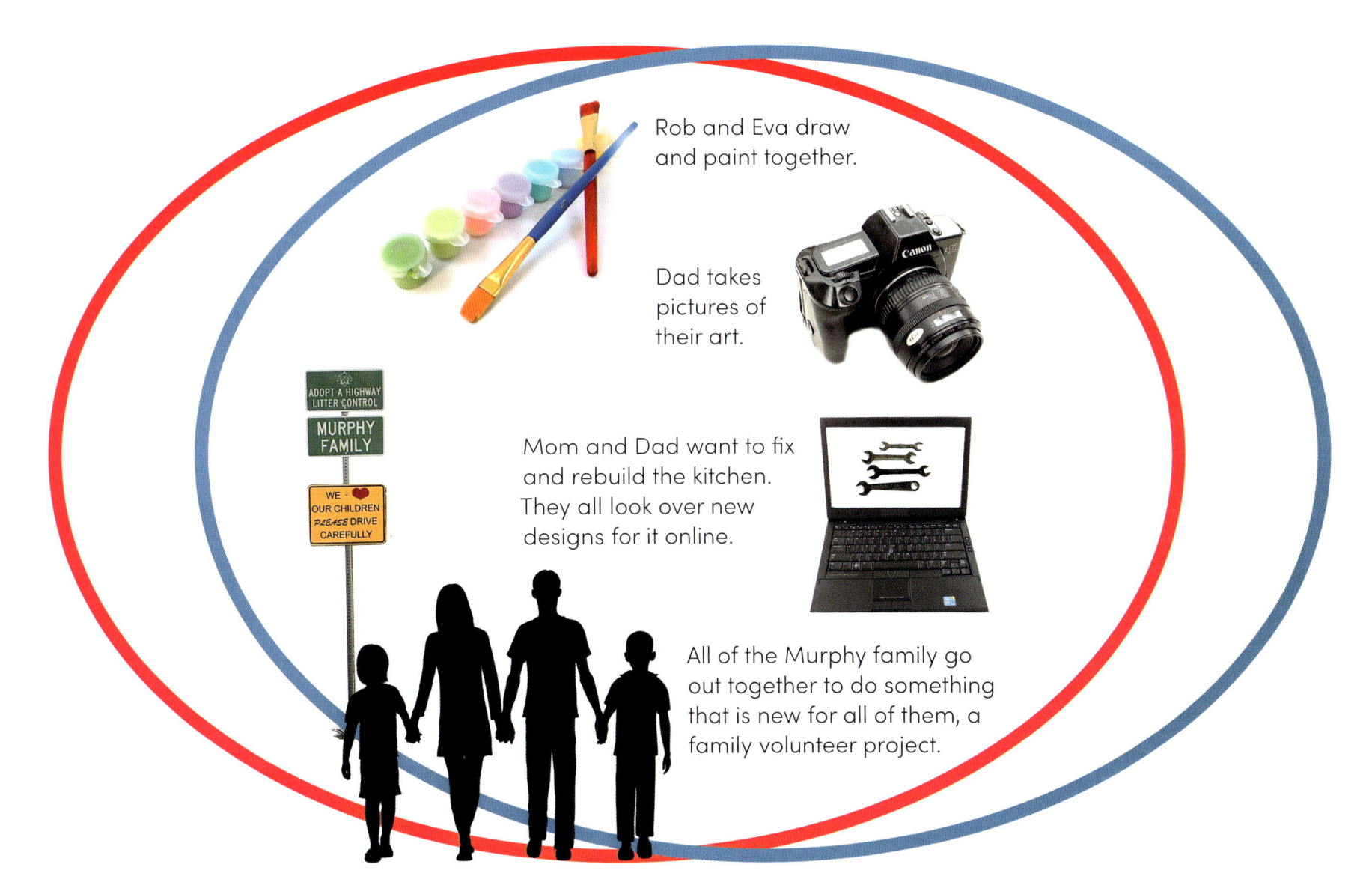

Rob and Eva draw and paint together.

Dad takes pictures of their art.

Mom and Dad want to fix and rebuild the kitchen. They all look over new designs for it online.

All of the Murphy family go out together to do something that is new for all of them, a family volunteer project.

Help Rob to join in activities with his family

1. You pretend to be Rob, and have a grown-up pretend to be different members of the family.
2. Create conversations in which Rob asks to do things with his family.

Would you like to _____?

Can I _____ with you?

I don't know much about _____. Can you tell me about it?

Can I hang out with you while you _____?

Can we take turns doing things we like? First maybe we can _____ and then maybe we can _____.

52

Practice talking with family and relatives

Now, pretend you are talking to someone in your own family.

1. Pick out a family member to pretend to talk with.
2. Talk with that person. Have the adult with you pretend to be the family member you picked out.

> Would you like to _____?
>
> Can I _____ with you?
>
> I don't know much about _____.
> Can you tell me about it?
>
> Can I hang out with you while you
> _____?
>
> Can we take turns doing things we like? First maybe we can _____ and then maybe we can _____.
>
> Are you busy now? Can we
> _____?
>
> Would you be able to help me with
> _____?
>
> Do you need any help with _____?
>
> When you were my age, what did you like doing for fun?
>
> Do you remember when we went to
> _____?
>
> Are we going there again?

THE FAMILY INTEREST EXPLORER PAGE

Here are lots of pictures showing things adults, teens or younger kids in your home might like.

1. Pick out things that seem important to certain people in your home.
2. Describe which ones you might be able to do sometimes with a family member.
3. Describe which things you could try to talk about with a family member:

Helping	Outdoor fun	TV	Movies	School, homework	Exercise	Video games	Other games
Listening to music	Making music	Phone	Computer, tablet	Pets	Making things	Travel	Making food
Eating good food	Shopping	Reading	Parties	Relaxing	Being with family	Being with relatives	Friends
People my family know	Housework	Yard work	Home improvements	Fixing things	News	Job	Adult hobby
Looking good	Old memories	Social media	Our hometown	Church, mosque, temple	Playing sports	Watching sports	Holidays CHRISTMAS! HANUKKAH! NEW YEARS! EASTER!

Family members and what they like to do

Write the names of four family members you live with or relatives you feel close to. Draw small pictures or write words to show what these people like to do.

Name:	Name:
Name:	Name:

Things I can do with family and relatives

When you are hanging out or playing with a family member or relative, sometimes the activity will be something you mainly like. Other times it may be something that the other person mainly likes. And still other times, the activity might be something that you both like the same. Make pictures or write words to show what activities you can do with a family member or relative.

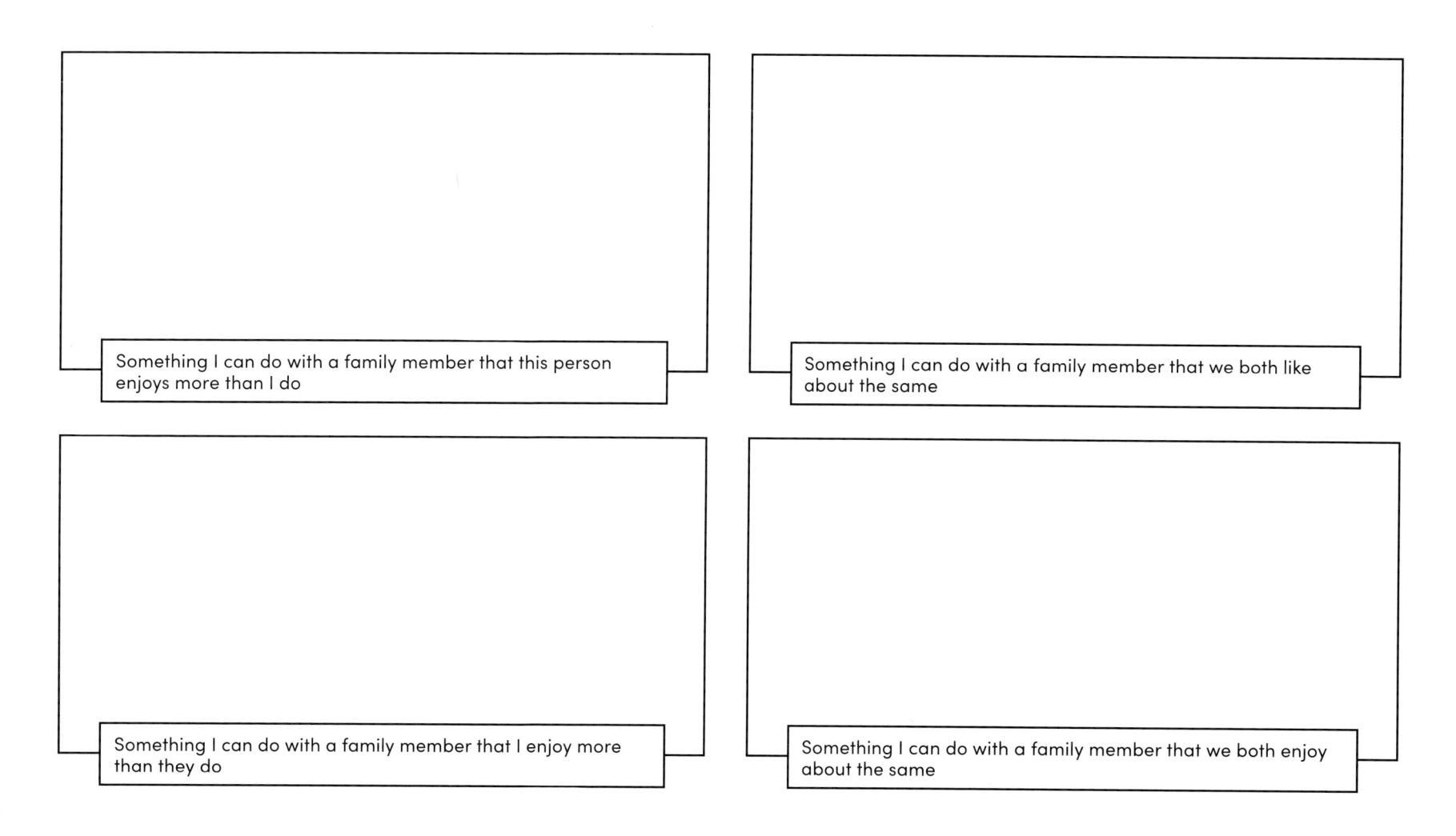

Something I can do with a family member that this person enjoys more than I do	Something I can do with a family member that we both like about the same
Something I can do with a family member that I enjoy more than they do	Something I can do with a family member that we both enjoy about the same

PART 5
JON AND THE VISITOR

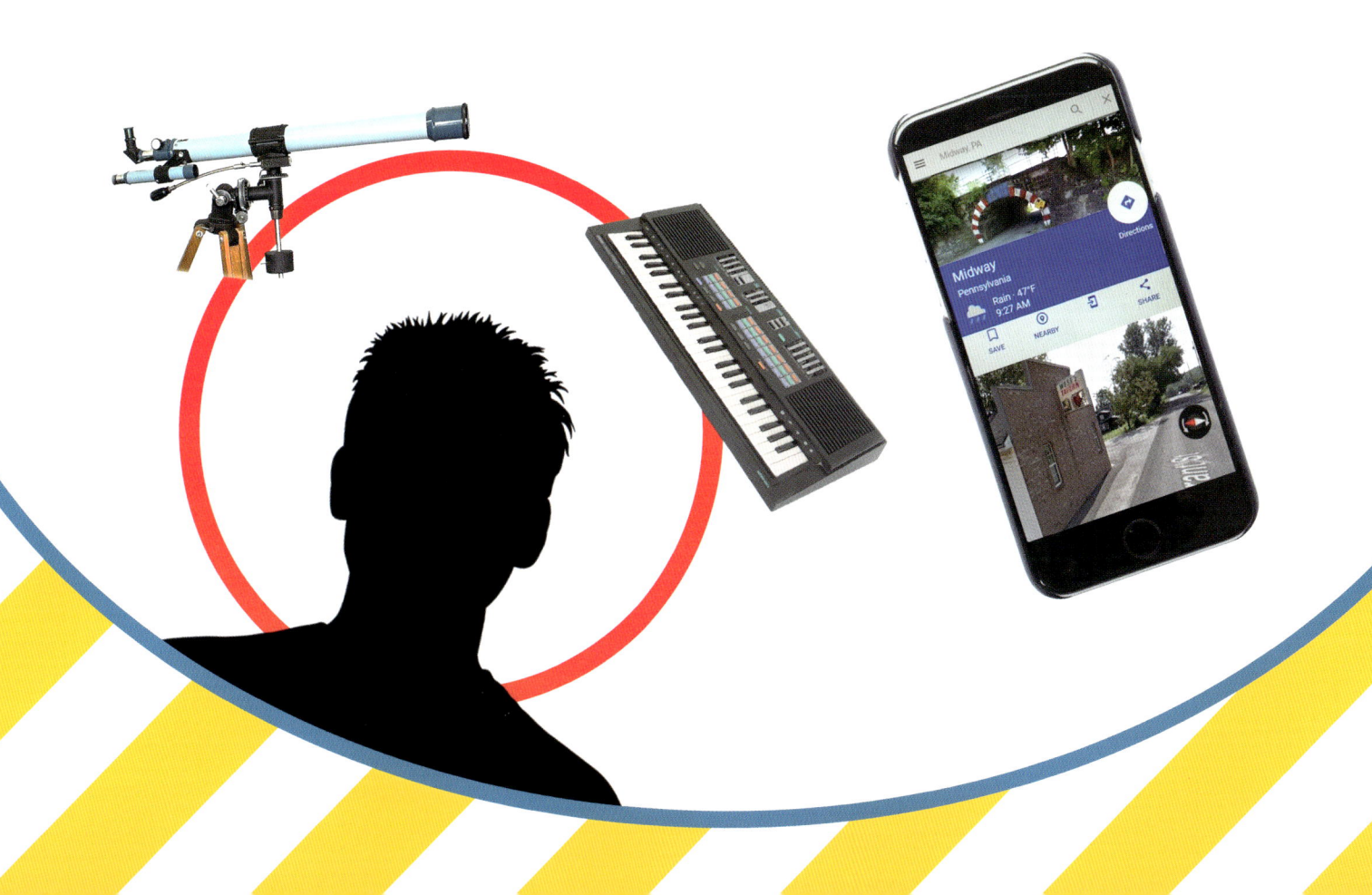

Jon hangs out with some young people at school in the lunchroom.

Dan, one of the kids from school, is going to come over to Jon's house.

This has Jon pretty worried. Jon is not used to being with people at home other than his mother.

At home, Jon is used to doing things his own special way.

Jon likes to sit in his chair, hold stuffed animals and watch TV.

Jon plays his two electric pianos. He can learn new songs without reading the music.

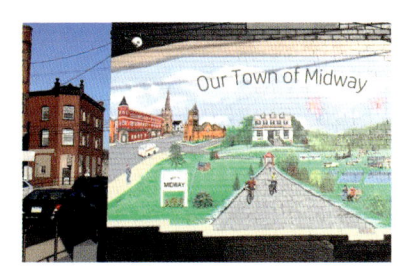

Jon likes to learn about space. He has a telescope he uses at night sometimes.

Jon sometimes likes to walk around his town.

Dan likes science. He likes fossils, and looking at things with this microscope.

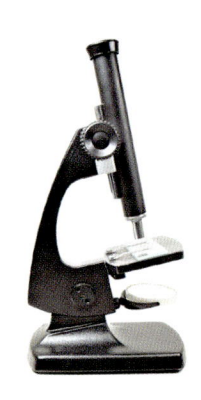

Dan

Dan likes music. He's not bad at singing. He has fixed up an old record player. He can make music on his computer.

Dan likes to explore his town and learn some things about it.

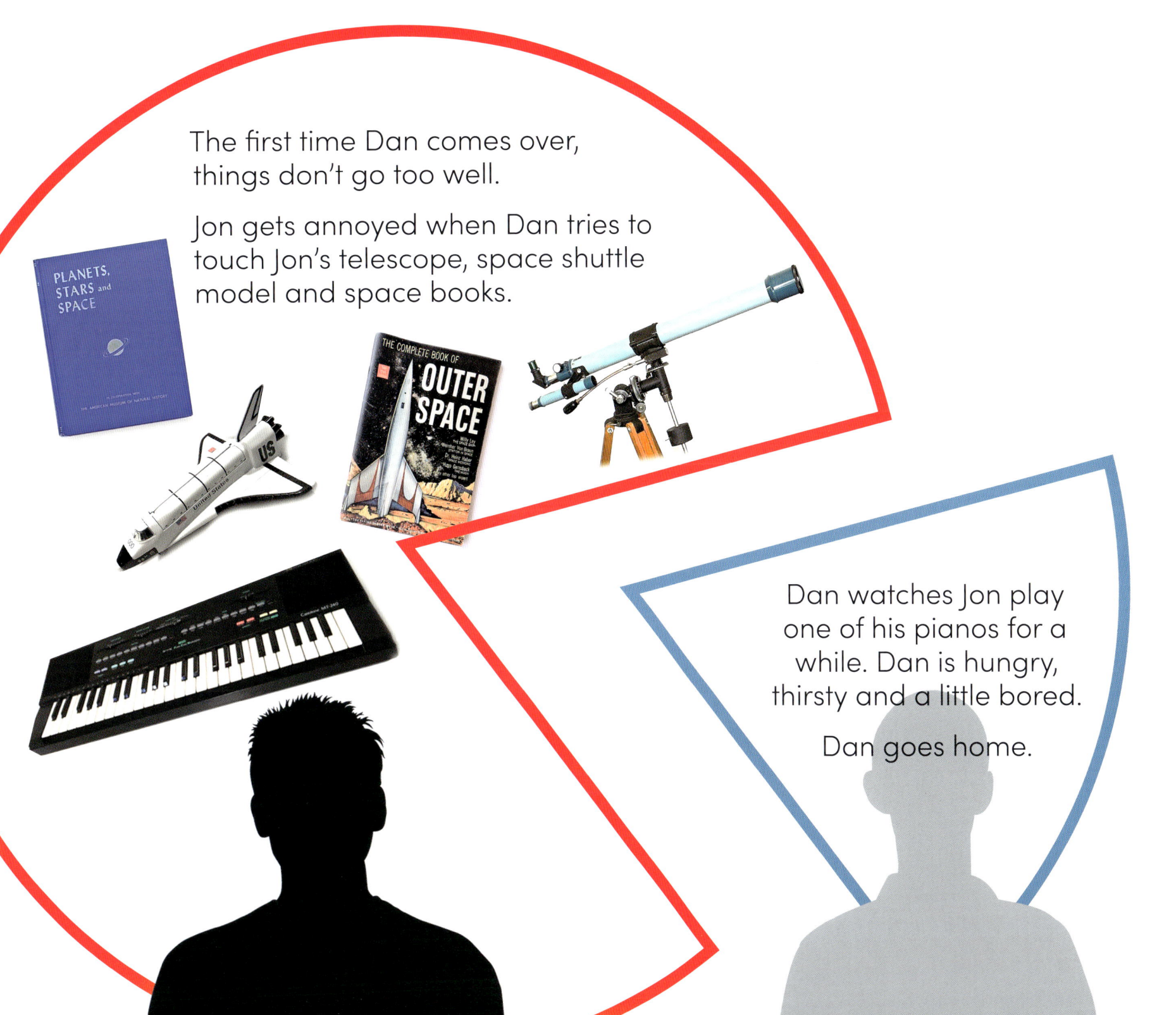

The first time Dan comes over, things don't go too well.

Jon gets annoyed when Dan tries to touch Jon's telescope, space shuttle model and space books.

Dan watches Jon play one of his pianos for a while. Dan is hungry, thirsty and a little bored.

Dan goes home.

To get along better, they can take turns. That way, each boy gets some of what he needs.

The second time Dan comes over, Jon asks Dan to show him how to create piano music on his tablet.

Jon gets out something for them to eat and drink.

They go out bowling, something they both enjoy.

The third time Dan and Jon get together, they walk around their town. First, they go to the library, Jon's favorite place. Then they go to the toy store, Dan's favorite place.

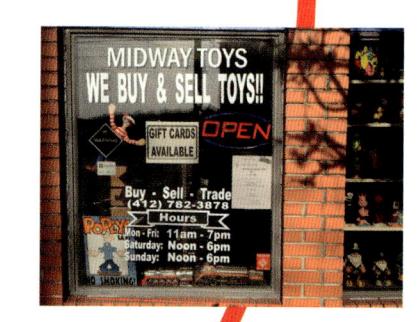

INSIDE THE HOME WHEN SOMEONE COMES OVER

There are so many choices. Be ready to try different things.

Show
- Around your home
- Family and pets
- Things you own

Games
- Video games
- Board/card games

Create
- Art
- Build
- Things on computer

Work
- Homework
- Other work, if they ask to help

Toys

Pretend play

Watch
- TV
- Movie
- Take turns looking at things on the computer

Eat and drink
- Snack
- Meal

OUTSIDE THE HOME WHEN SOMEONE COMES OVER

Walk, run, ride	Throw, catch	Playground, park	Go to watch
Sit around	Outdoor action	See neighborhood, town	Pay to play

When someone comes over – things to do indoors

When someone comes over, they are looking forward to doing things that they like and not just what you like. Pick out four indoor activities that your visitor might enjoy. Draw pictures of these or just write the words.

For this worksheet, only ONE activity may be on a screen (video game, computer, TV, etc.).

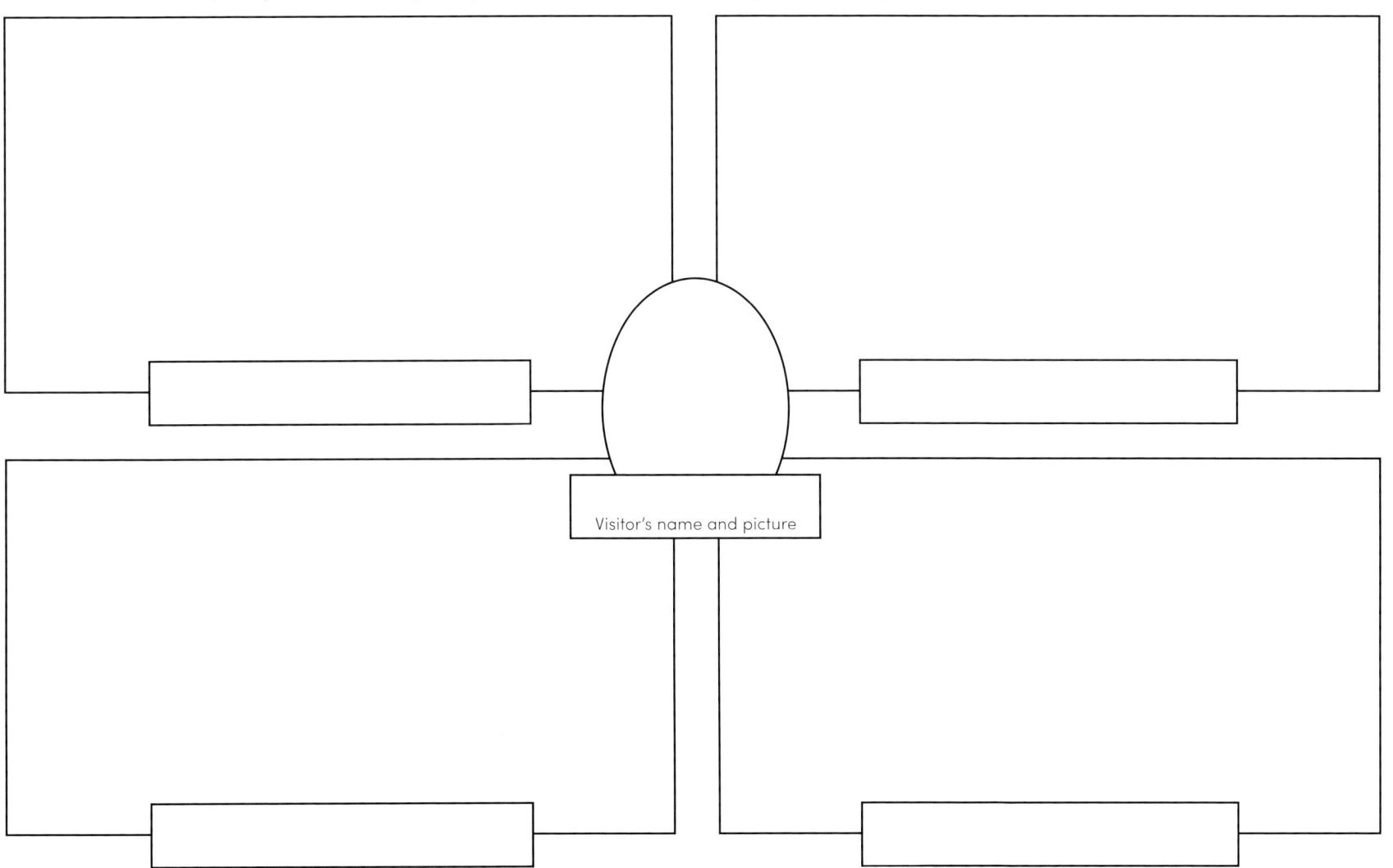

Visitor's name and picture

When someone comes over – things to do outdoors

When someone comes over, they are looking forward to doing things that they like and not just what you like. Pick out four outdoor activities (on your property, or in your neighborhood or town) that your visitor might enjoy. Draw pictures of these or just write the words.

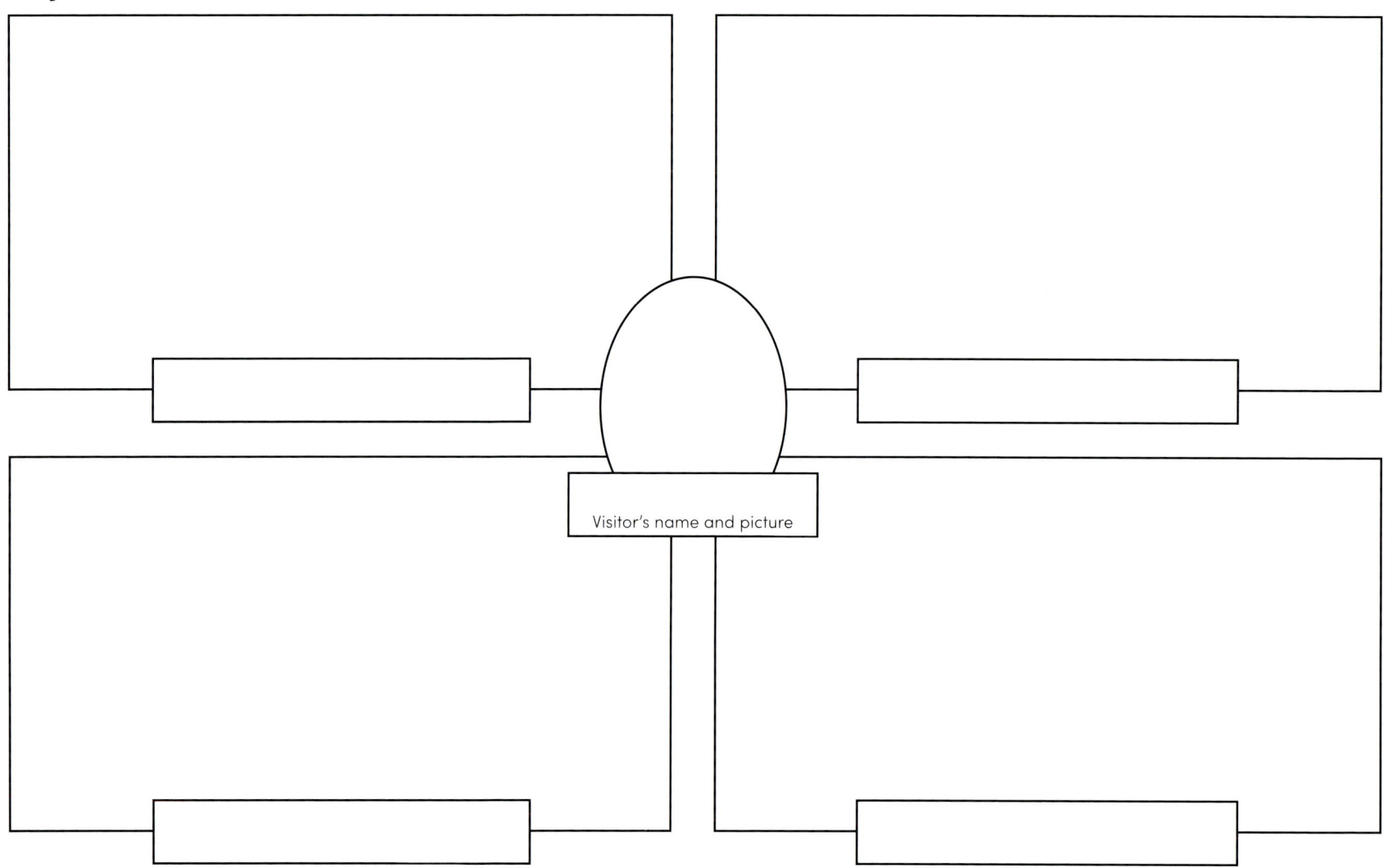

Visitor's name and picture

PART 6
ALAN AND GROWING UP SO FAST

When Alan finds something he likes, he sticks with it for years. Mostly, that's fine.

There is a certain pillow he likes more than any other, ever since he was little.

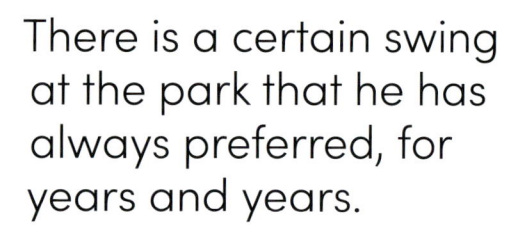

There is a certain swing at the park that he has always preferred, for years and years.

There is just one bowl and one spoon he likes for eating his cereal in the morning, and no other bowl or spoon will do.

But over time, some of Alan's young interests have become unusual...

...because other people his age have moved on to new interests.

Alan still watches lots of little kid shows...

...while others his age often watch shows about things that are more mature.

At the park, Alan sits right down with little kids to play in the sand...

...while other kids his age are talking and thinking about more grown-up things.

Alan still mainly likes pretend things...

...while others his age, more and more, are into real things.

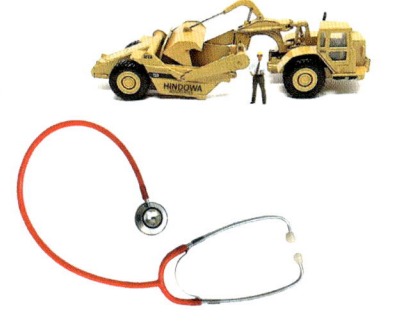

At school, and at his after-school program, Alan is starting to have problems.

Alan is getting big. When he tries to play with littler and younger kids, they sometimes get confused or annoyed.

A few of the kids that are Alan's age really do like Alan and want to hang out with him. But more and more, they don't like Alan's little kid toys, games and activities.

Help Alan to find more "big kid" activities

Imagine that you are one of Alan's teachers, helping him to get better at playing and talking with kids his age. Below are a number of things that Alan likes. Which of them are common interests for 13-year-olds? Place a circle around these boxes. Which seem a bit young for someone that age – things that might be better to do alone at home? Put a check ✓ in these circles.

○ Pretending to be cops and robbers	○ YouTube videos of dancing vegetables	○ Watching a show about the world's biggest airplanes	○ Hitting a balloon back and forth
○ Making paper airplanes and throwing them around	○ Learning about someone's family	○ Talking about the newest and best phones	○ Watching a show about talking trains
○ Playing Follow the Leader	○ Drawing pictures of trains	○ Pretending to be dinosaurs	○ Playing catch with a ball

Help yourself. Do you need to learn more play activities that are better for older kids?

Everyone, even many adults, likes to do some "little kid" things. But as we get older, we should also learn to do things and talk about things that others our age enjoy.

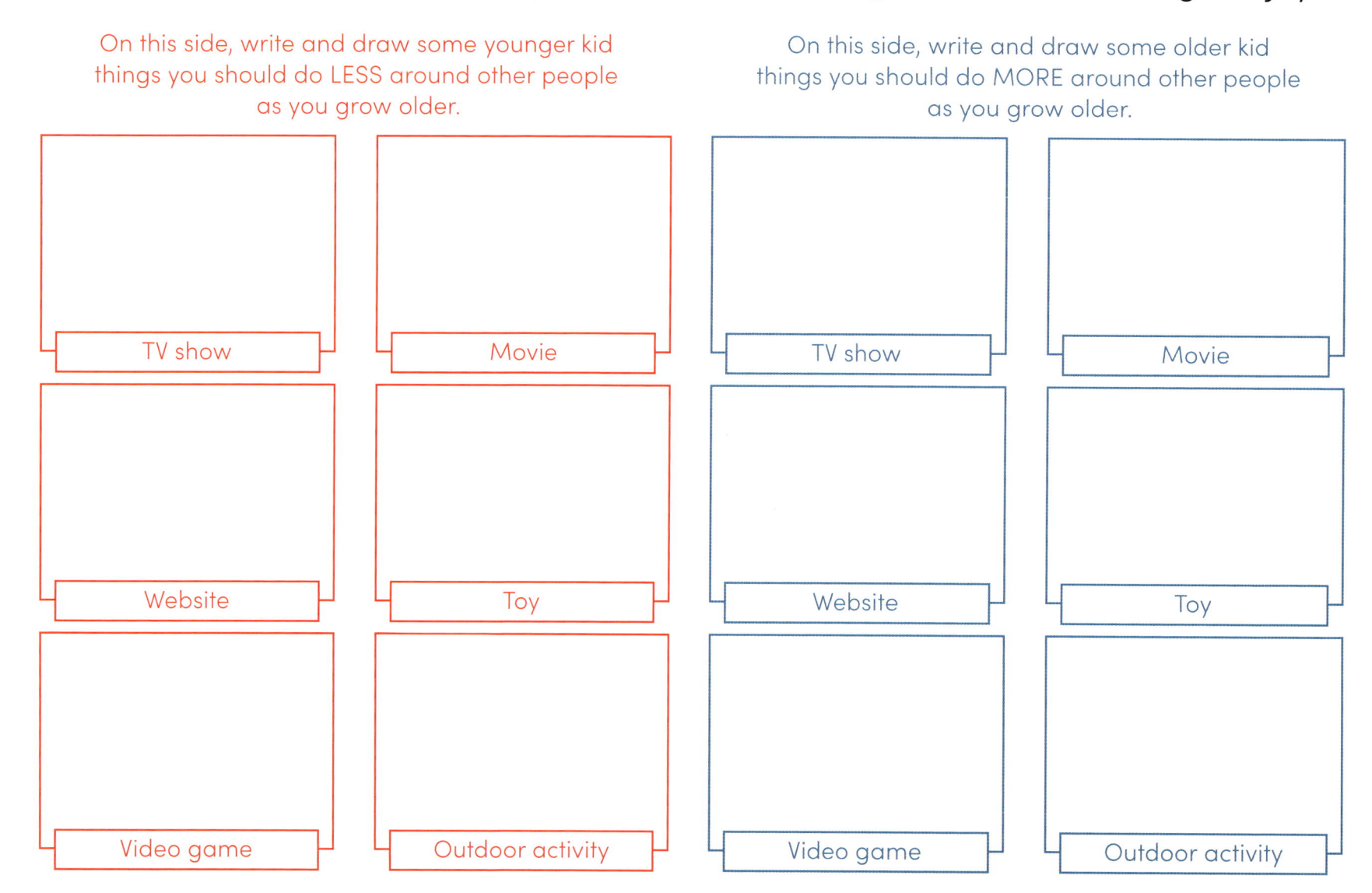

On this side, write and draw some younger kid things you should do LESS around other people as you grow older.

On this side, write and draw some older kid things you should do MORE around other people as you grow older.

TV show	Movie	TV show	Movie
Website	Toy	Website	Toy
Video game	Outdoor activity	Video game	Outdoor activity

PART 7

WHEN HANGING OUT AND PLAYING IS HARD

IT'S HARD AT FIRST. THEN IT GETS BETTER

Everyone can get better at hanging out and playing. But people can run into problems along the way. In this part, you can learn how to cope with some of these problems and enjoy people even more.

Jeff relies too much on his special interest to stay calm.

Sara worries about what might happen and what people might think.

Ana has problems with certain loud sounds and crowded places.

Rob gets stubborn and grouchy if he can't do what he wants.

Jon misses his home if he is away for too long.

Alan gets discouraged about himself and worried about his future.

For Jeff, it's hard at first.

I feel nervous and restless when I can't do my favorite thing all the time.

The things that other kids like seem confusing or boring to me.

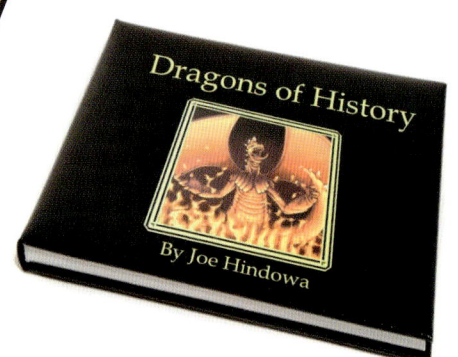

I honestly do not really feel lonely – except when I am away from my dragons.

It can get much better.

People can try different ways of thinking.

People can try different ways of doing things.

What might be helpful for Jeff?

Which might be helpful for you?

I will still have lots of time to do my favorite thing alone, even after I do other activities.

Some things other people like might be okay – I have not even tried them very much yet.

Many things seem hard and scary until you get used to them.

For Sara, it's hard at first.

If I try to play with other kids, how will I know for sure what is going to happen?

If things don't go well, will other kids think bad things about me?

Maybe I should just play it safe and hang out at home.

It can get much better.

People can try different ways of thinking.

People can try different ways of doing things.

What might be helpful for Sara?

Which might be helpful for you?

A person should learn to get ready for some new things to happen that they were not expecting.

I already spend enough time alone. Playing with other kids might be fun. It will be good for me.

It's true that other people will remember things about me and talk about me. Some things they say might be nice.

For Ana, it's hard at first.

I just can't deal with annoying sounds in some parts of my home and in many public places.

When places get crowded, loud or smelly, I just have to get away.

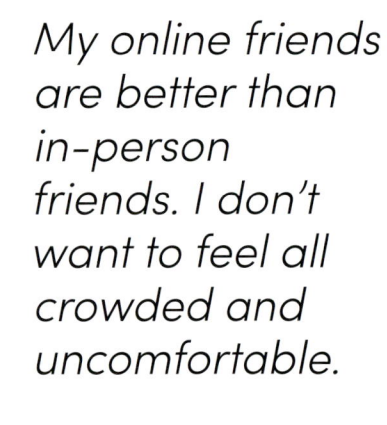

My online friends are better than in-person friends. I don't want to feel all crowded and uncomfortable.

It can get much better.

People can try different ways of thinking.

People can try different ways of doing things.

What might be helpful for Ana?

Which might be helpful for you?

I can try some different ways to block out loud or unwanted sounds.

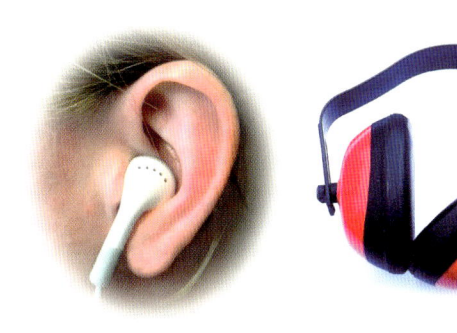

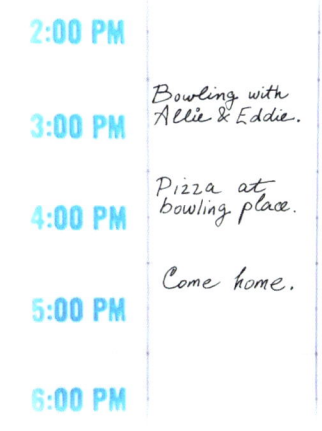

I can get used to being around groups of people a little at a time.

I can plan breaks and plenty of time to rest.

I can keep some online friends, but I can make my real friends more important.

For Rob, it's hard at first.

My mind works best when I play with building toys alone. Why should I try new things I can't do well?

I am going to miss my Lego® a lot if I start doing more stuff with my family and other kids.

My building toys are like friends to me. I don't really feel lonely for people.

It can get much better.

People can try different ways of thinking.

People can try different ways of doing things.

What might be helpful for Rob?

Which might be helpful for you?

People shouldn't spend all their time alone doing one thing. I can teach my brain new things.

If I am away from my building toys a while, I will miss them some. But it might be good for me. And it will certainly be good for my family.

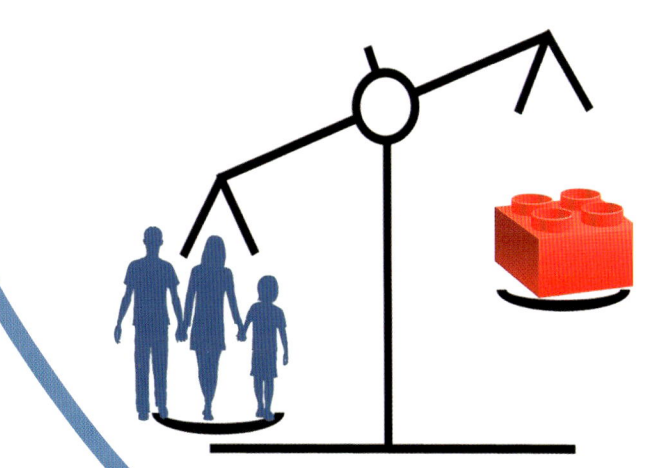

If I am starting to like things like Lego® more than people, that's a problem I may need to work on.

83

For Jon, it's hard at first.

The last time I was away from my home for a few hours, I missed my home so much.

It's hard to be away from my mom when I'm in a strange place.

Other places don't seem comfortable like my home is.

It can get much better.

People can try different ways of thinking.

People can try different ways of doing things.

What might be helpful for Jon?

Which might be helpful for you?

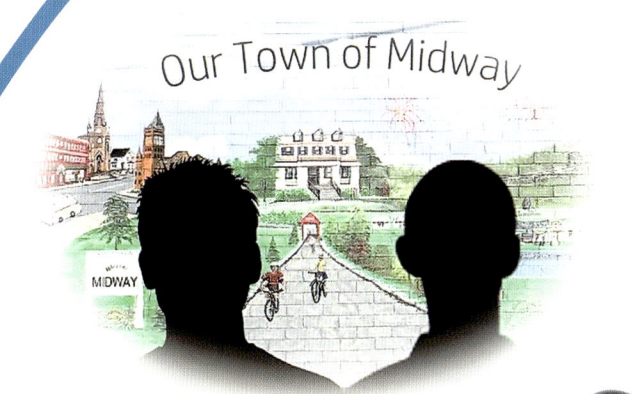

With a friend, my town might start to feel like home, too.

People can get used to being away from their parents if they keep trying.

Think: The comforts of home will still be there later.

For Alan, it's hard at first.

Many days I just don't like myself much. It's hard to hang out with people when I feel that way.

I am afraid to even start spending more time with people my age.

Some kids are so mean to me!

Others ignore me.

Will I ever fit in?

It can get much better.

People can try different ways of thinking.

People can try different ways of doing things.

What might be helpful for Alan?

Which might be helpful for you?

If I try to treat people well, some will find things to like about me.

If I feel afraid or stuck, there may be people who can help me.

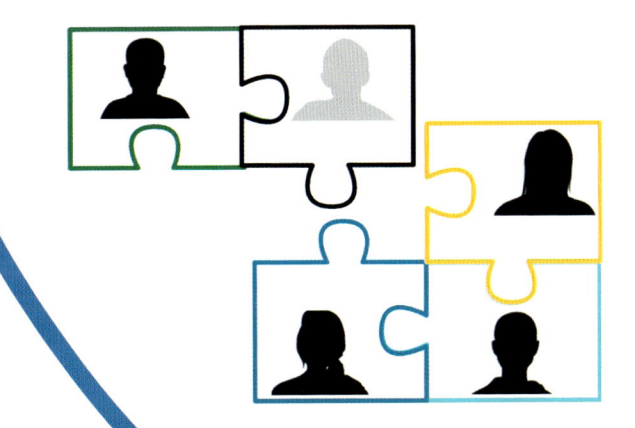

Maybe I won't fit in with lots of people. Probably I will fit in with some.

When playing is hard – a checklist

Having someone over, or going to someone's house, can be great. But it can also be hard sometimes. It is important to know what might go wrong so you can get ready for it.

Put a check next to the ones that are hard for you sometimes.

At someone else's house – what things are difficult?

I feel nervous before going ○	I miss my parents when I am away ○
Different food I don't like ○	Weird sounds in other people's homes ○
Different rules ○	Different music I don't like ○
Other people make me mad ○	Other kids show up who I was not expecting ○
I miss my home when I am away ○	Using other people's bathrooms ○
I am too hot or too cold ○	Different video games I don't know ○
When the plan for playing changes ○	If I lose at games ○
It lasts too long and I want to go home ○	Weird smell in other people's homes ○

When someone comes over – what things are difficult?

I feel worried before the person arrives ○	I sometimes want them to leave after they arrive ○
The visitor doesn't know my home's rules ○	Playing gets loud and confusing ○
The visitor doesn't want to watch me play ○	Arguing with the visitor ○
It's my house and I feel I should be in charge ○	I want to play alone and the visitor won't let me ○
The visitor touches things that are mine ○	The visitor plays with my brother or sister instead of just me ○
The visitor brings something to play with I don't like ○	The visitor brings a video game I don't like ○
The visitor is bored and I don't know why ○	The visitor doesn't know I do certain things at certain times of day ○
The visitor talks when I just want to have quiet ○	The visitor wants to invite other kids to play who I don't like ○

Hard things when someone comes over and things that can help

Pick three things that are the very hardest for you about having someone come over to play. On the right, write down some things you can do about it. Draw little pictures too if you like. Copy this page if you need more space for your ideas.

😕 Hard for me when someone comes over to play: 🙂 Things I might do to make it better:

Hard things when I visit friends and things that can help

Pick three things that are the hardest when you hang out with friends.

On the right, write down some things you can do about it. Draw little pictures too if you like. Copy this page if you need more space for your ideas.

😕 Hard for me when I visit friends: 🙂 Things I might do to make it better:

Like the people in this book, you too can find good ways to spend time with people.

You can keep enjoying the things you love, and your time by yourself.

Playing and hanging out will be hard sometimes. But as you learn about other people, and the interests you share with them, you may enjoy it more and more.

THANKS FOR VISITING
MIDWAY
~ Come again soon! ~

PART 8

HELP 32 PEOPLE TO PLAY AND HANG OUT!

On the next eight pages, you will find lots of people trying to find good ways to enjoy being around other people.

There are so many ways that their playing and hanging out can go well, or not so well!

Read the directions at the top of each page and have fun!

Help James figure out how to talk, play and hang out with his relatives

James has been spending a lot of time by himself. He is trying to spend more time with relatives.

1. Describe what James can do or say with each relative that is in some way connected to his own interests.
2. Describe what he can do or say to show interest in something that is outside of his interests.
3. Describe some mistakes that James might make – ways he might talk or play that do not connect him to his relatives.

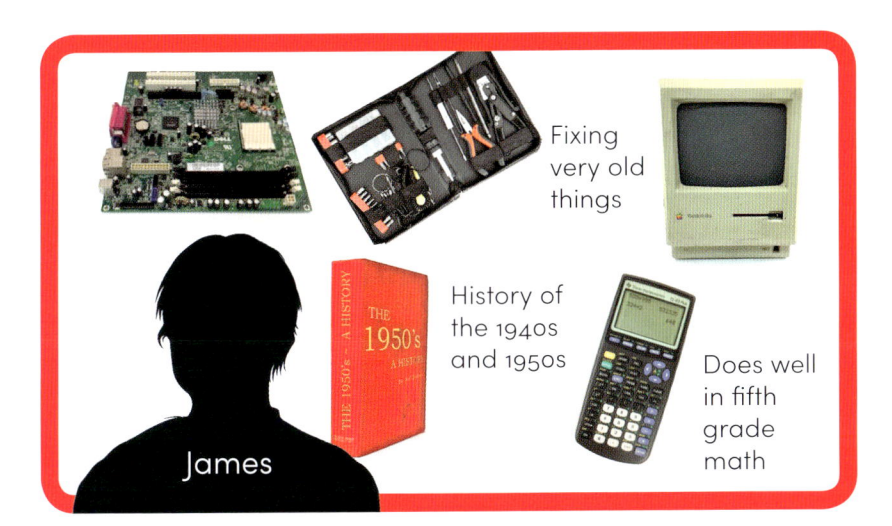

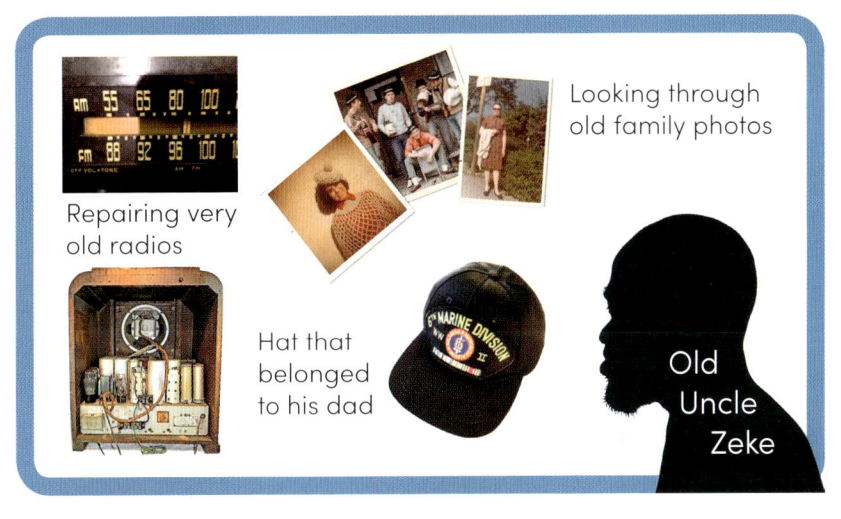

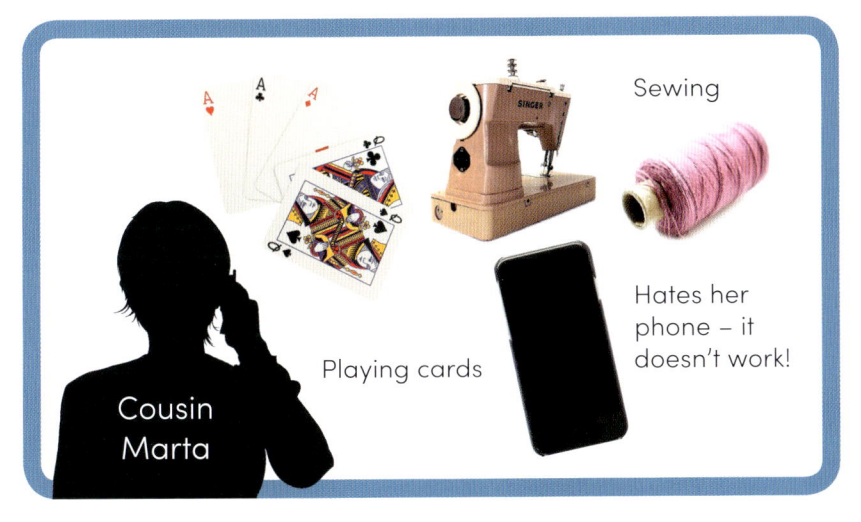

James
- Fixing very old things
- History of the 1940s and 1950s
- Does well in fifth grade math

Old Uncle Zeke
- Repairing very old radios
- Looking through old family photos
- Hat that belonged to his dad

Cousin Marta
- Playing cards
- Sewing
- Hates her phone – it doesn't work!

Cousin Jill
- Trying to learn how to play some games
- Trying to do well in first-grade math

93

Help Cody figure out how to talk, play and hang out with his relatives

Cody just moved to a city where he has lots more relatives nearby. He is trying to find ways to spend time with them.

1. Describe what Cody can do or say with each relative that is in some way connected to his own interests.
2. Describe what Cody can do or say to show interest in something that is outside of his interests.
3. Describe some mistakes that Cody might make – ways he might talk or play that do not connect him to his relatives.

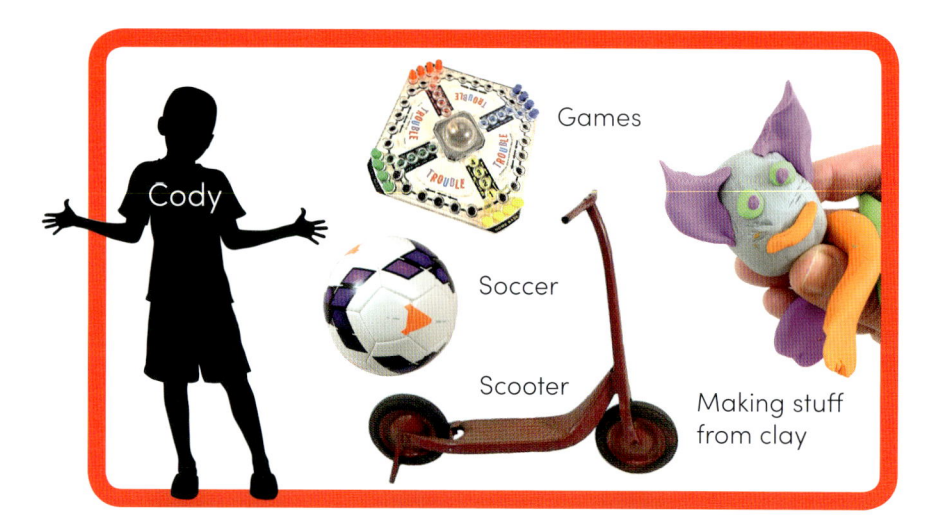

Cody: Games, Soccer, Scooter, Making stuff from clay

Aunt Lou: Pottery, Long walks, Cooking for people

Cousin Frank: Playing with his plastic animals and his planes, Pretending to be a cowboy, Wants someone to show him how to throw, Stuffed animals

Great Grandma: Remembering Cody's great grandpa, Games, Fishing

Help Jake figure out how to talk, play and hang out with his relatives

Jake is just starting to find out how to enjoy spending time with his relatives.

1. Describe what Jake can do or say with each relative that is in some way connected to his own interests.
2. Describe what he can do or say to show interest in something that is outside of his interests.
3. Describe some mistakes that Jake might make – ways of playing that do not connect him to his relatives.

Jake
- Reading this for school
- Reading this for fun
- His toy cars
- Trying to learn how to play this
- Collects squirt guns

Aunt Beth
- Her horses
- Her work

Cousin Joe
- Playing pool
- Water fun outside
- What he likes to read
- Skateboarding

Uncle Bill
- His work
- Old books about monsters and heroes
- Has played this thing since he was a kid

Help Shania figure out how to talk, play and hang out with her relatives

Since Shania's mom got a job, Shania ends up spending lots more time with relatives while her mom is at work.

1. Describe what Shania can do or say with each relative that is in some way connected to her own interests.
2. Describe what she can do or say to show interest in something that is outside of her interests.
3. Describe some mistakes that Shania might make – ways she might talk or play that do not connect her to her relatives.

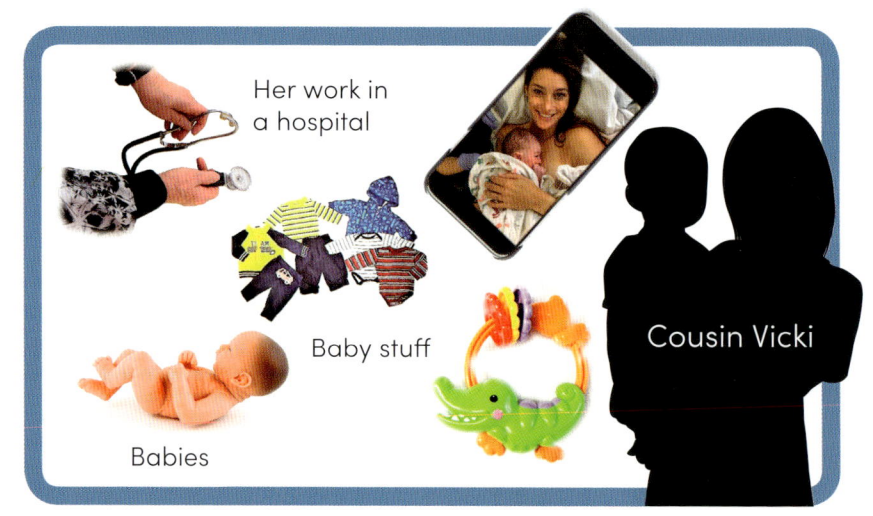

Shania: Painting, How to become a doctor, Foreign countries, Making signs

Aunt Lil: Making art, Art supplies, Her sign shop

Uncle Al: Faraway places, Camping in national parks

Cousin Vicki: Her work in a hospital, Baby stuff, Babies

Create matches and figure out how these people can hang out and play

1. Describe playing that goes badly! Make up stories about how any two, three or four of these kids get together and they don't take turns or find what they have in common.
2. Make up stories about any get-togethers that go well, with kids taking turns and finding what they all like.
3. Make up stories about YOU getting together with any of these kids. How could it go well? How could it go badly?

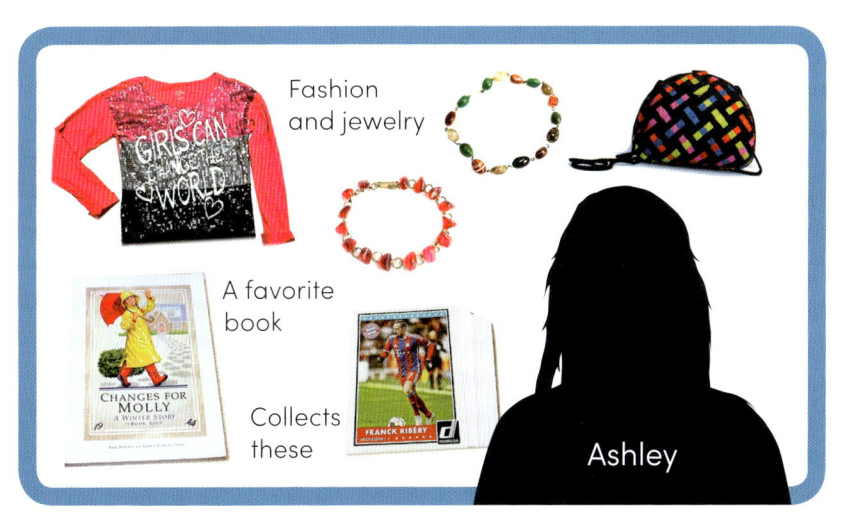

Imani
- Showing her drawings
- A doll she likes
- Looking nice
- Summer outfits

Vinh
- Learning to draw
- Toy cars
- Has 200 of these cards
- Dinosaurs

Sean
- Brings this book everywhere
- World news
- Collects these

Ashley
- Fashion and jewelry
- A favorite book
- Collects these

Create matches and figure out how these people can hang out and play

1. Describe playing that goes badly! Make up stories about how any two, three or four of these kids get together and they don't take turns or find what they have in common.
2. Make up stories about any get-togethers that go well, with kids taking turns and finding what they all like.
3. Make up stories about YOU getting together with any of these kids. How could it go well? How could it go badly?

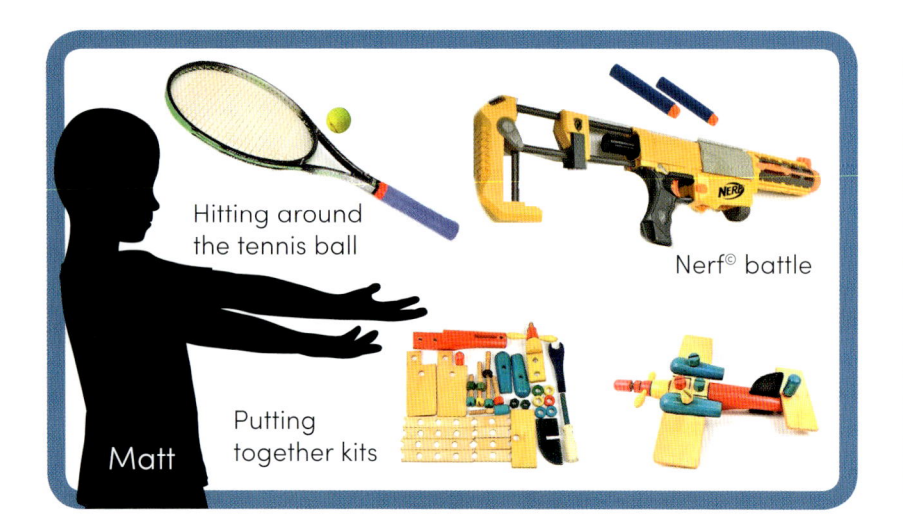

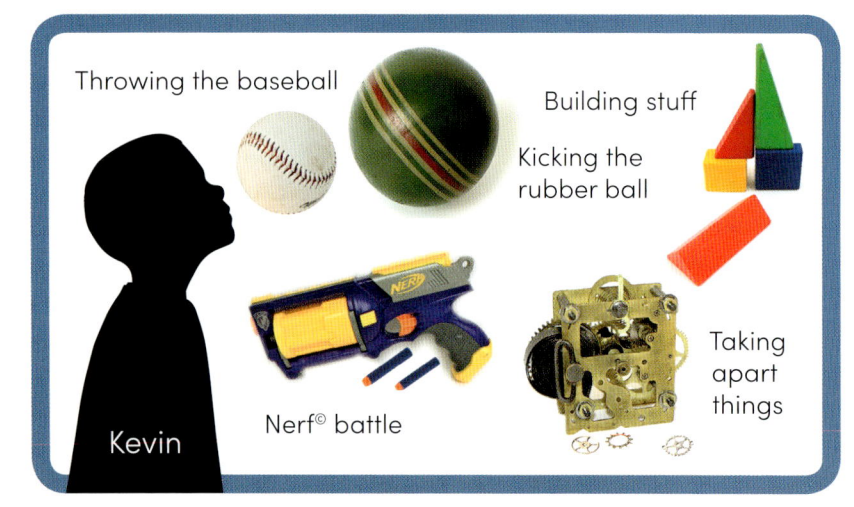

Matt
- Hitting around the tennis ball
- Nerf© battle
- Putting together kits

Lamar
- Playing with the trains
- Playing with the wagon
- Making something with his tools
- Playing football

Kevin
- Throwing the baseball
- Building stuff
- Kicking the rubber ball
- Nerf© battle
- Taking apart things

Tanner
- Organizing his shell collection
- Playing hockey
- Police pretend play

98

Create matches and figure out how these people can hang out and play

1. Describe playing that goes badly! Make up stories about how any two, three or four of these kids get together and they don't take turns or find what they have in common.
2. Make up stories about any get-togethers that go well, with kids taking turns and finding what they all like.
3. Make up stories about YOU getting together with any of these kids. How could it go well? How could it go badly?

Emma
- Getting Grandpa's old radio to work
- Playing with her rabbit
- Dancing
- From Grandma's attic
- Playing this game in the yard

Ellie
- Sleeps with this
- Playing sports and collecting sports cards
- Playing with the dog
- Getting this old radio to work

Ava
- Playing with stuffed animals
- Playing pretend school
- Gifts from her uncle

Sophie
- Often wears this shirt
- A favorite book
- Likes ping-pong
- Trying to learn some Spanish

Create matches and figure out how these people can hang out and play

1. Describe playing that goes badly! Make up stories about how any two, three or four of these kids get together and they don't take turns or find what they have in common.
2. Make up stories about any get-togethers that go well, with kids taking turns and finding what they all like.
3. Make up stories about YOU getting together with any of these kids. How could it go well? How could it go badly?

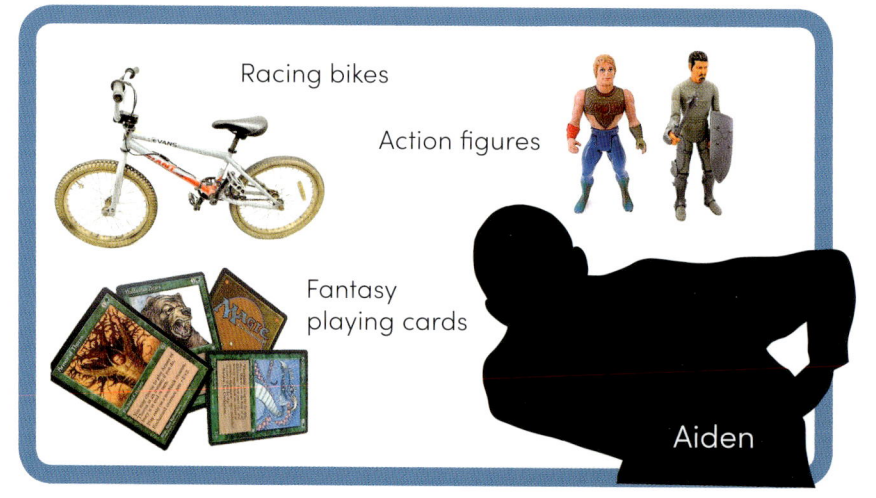

Jack
- Racing this car
- Old coins
- Halloween
- Bike repair
- Battles with these action figures

Liam
- Solving this cube
- Running this car
- Checking out cool birds
- Action figures from movies

Noah
- Riding bike to find nature stuff to collect
- Helping Dad with the bees
- Helping Mom sell vegetables

Aiden
- Racing bikes
- Action figures
- Fantasy playing cards

MORE FUN WAYS TO USE THESE PAGES

If you are reading this book with an adult, have the adult play the role of any of the 32 people in this part while you talk with them and make plans on how to play and hang out.

Just for fun! On pages 93 to 100, find:

- 5 signs
- 1 pen
- 4 phones
- 2 musical instruments
- 3 planes
- 3 pairs of shoes or boots
- 3 dogs
- 4 birds
- 24 balls
- 4 guns
- 4 old photos
- 3 shirts
- 3 hats
- 8 horseshoes
- 3 rabbits
- 3 bees

Pick any of the 32 people on these pages. If this was your own friend or relative, how would you play or hang out?

In the whole book – find 35 times the word "Midway" appears!

PART 9
More Activities, Games and Extension Activities

THE PLAY AND HANGING OUT CHALLENGE GAME

Show what you know about playing and hanging out. Find out what other people know.

Flip a coin to see if you answer the question or whether you get to ask one of the other players.

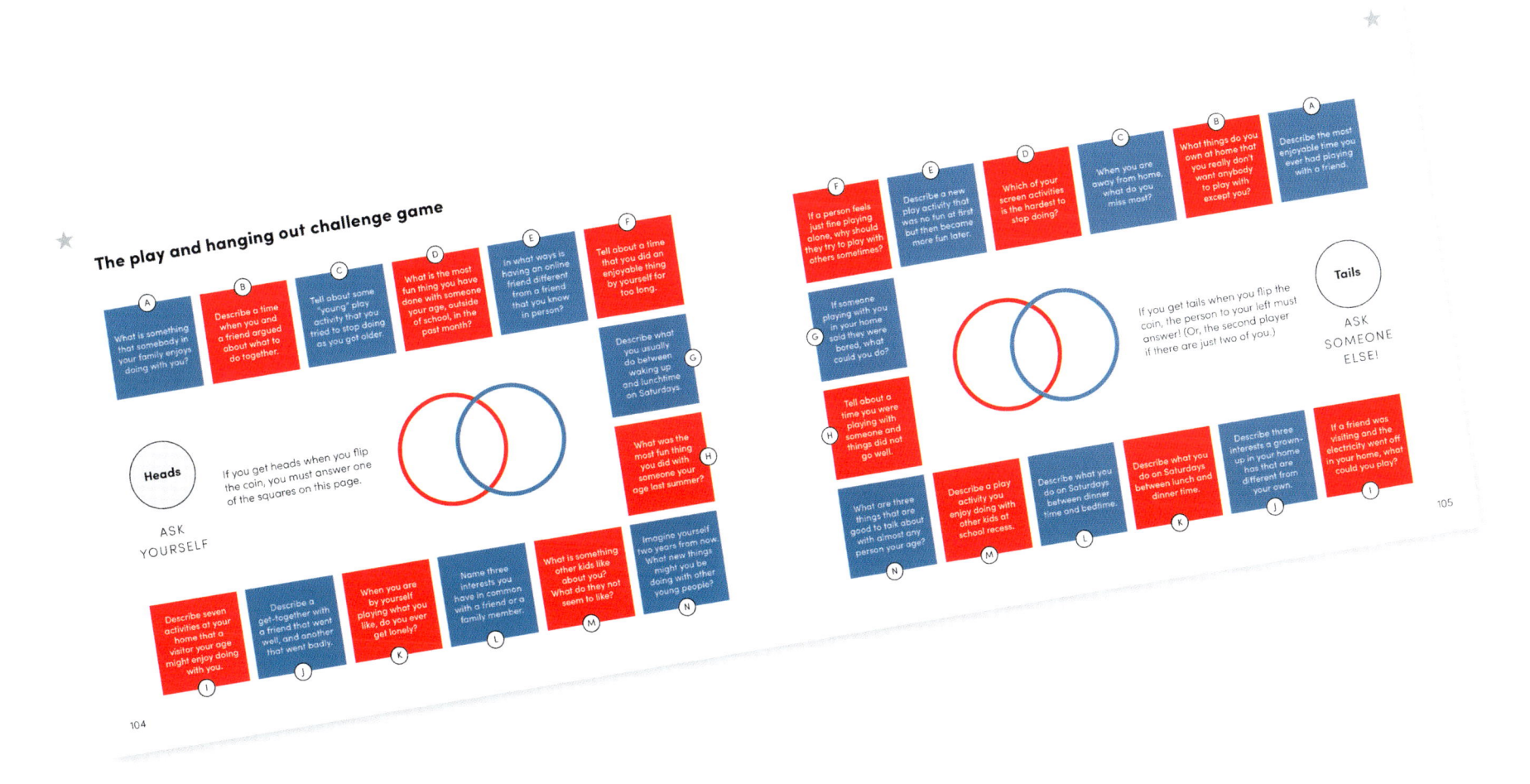

The play and hanging out challenge game

Heads — If you get heads when you flip the coin, you must answer one of the squares on this page.

ASK YOURSELF

Tails — If you get tails when you flip the coin, the person to your left must answer! (Or, the second player if there are just two of you.)

ASK SOMEONE ELSE!

- **A.** What is something that somebody in your family enjoys doing with you?
- **B.** Describe a time when you and a friend argued about what to do together.
- **C.** Tell about some "young" play activity that you tried to stop doing as you got older.
- **D.** What is the most fun thing you have done with someone your age, outside of school, in the past month?
- **E.** In what ways is having an online friend different from a friend that you know in person?
- **F.** Tell about a time that you did an enjoyable thing by yourself for too long.
- **G.** Describe what you usually do between waking up and lunchtime on Saturdays.
- **H.** What was the most fun thing you did with someone your age last summer?
- **I.** Describe seven activities at your home that a visitor your age might enjoy doing with you.
- **J.** Describe a get-together with a friend that went well, and another that went badly.
- **K.** When you are by yourself playing what you like, do you ever get lonely?
- **L.** Name three interests you have in common with a friend or a family member.
- **M.** What is something other kids like about you? What do they not seem to like?
- **N.** Imagine yourself two years from now. What new things might you be doing with other young people?

- **A.** Describe the most enjoyable time you ever had playing with a friend.
- **B.** What things do you own at home that you really don't want anybody to play with except you?
- **C.** When you are away from home, what do you miss most?
- **D.** Which of your screen activities is the hardest to stop doing?
- **E.** Describe a new play activity that was no fun at first but then became more fun later.
- **F.** If a person feels just fine playing alone, why should they try to play with others sometimes?
- **G.** If someone playing with you in your home said they were bored, what could you do?
- **H.** Tell about a time you were playing with someone and things did not go well.
- **I.** If a friend was visiting and the electricity went off in your home, what could you play?
- **J.** Describe three interests a grown-up in your home has that are different from your own.
- **K.** Describe what you do on Saturdays between lunch and dinner time.
- **L.** Describe what you do on Saturdays between dinner time and bedtime.
- **M.** Describe a play activity you enjoy doing with other kids at school recess.
- **N.** What are three things that are good to talk about with almost any person your age?

The play and hanging out challenge game

A. What is something that somebody in your family enjoys doing with you?

B. Describe a time when you and a friend argued about what to do together.

C. Tell about some "young" play activity that you tried to stop doing as you got older.

D. What is the most fun thing you have done with someone your age, outside of school, in the past month?

E. In what ways is having an online friend different from a friend that you know in person?

F. Tell about a time that you did an enjoyable thing by yourself for too long.

Heads

ASK YOURSELF

If you get heads when you flip the coin, you must answer one of the squares on this page.

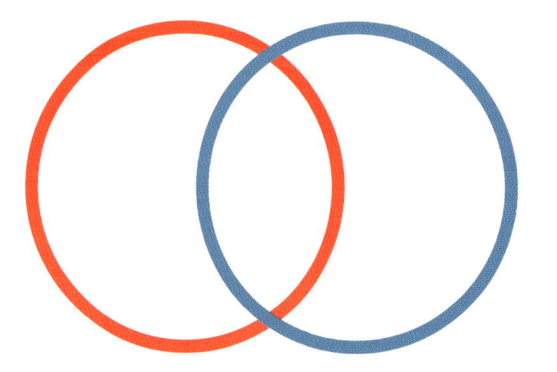

G. Describe what you usually do between waking up and lunchtime on Saturdays.

H. What was the most fun thing you did with someone your age last summer?

I. Describe seven activities at your home that a visitor your age might enjoy doing with you.

J. Describe a get-together with a friend that went well, and another that went badly.

K. When you are by yourself playing what you like, do you ever get lonely?

L. Name three interests you have in common with a friend or a family member.

M. What is something other kids like about you? What do they not seem to like?

N. Imagine yourself two years from now. What new things might you be doing with other young people?

F — If a person feels just fine playing alone, why should they try to play with others sometimes?

E — Describe a new play activity that was no fun at first but then became more fun later.

D — Which of your screen activities is the hardest to stop doing?

C — When you are away from home, what do you miss most?

B — What things do you own at home that you really don't want anybody to play with except you?

A — Describe the most enjoyable time you ever had playing with a friend.

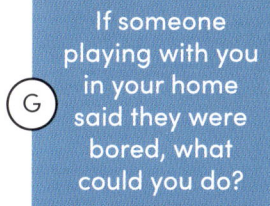

G — If someone playing with you in your home said they were bored, what could you do?

H — Tell about a time you were playing with someone and things did not go well.

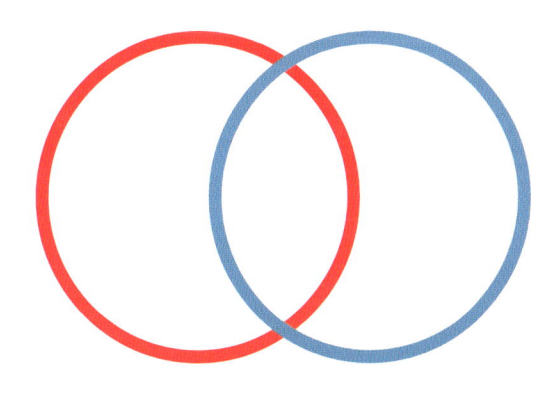

If you get tails when you flip the coin, the person to your left must answer! (Or, the second player if there are just two of you.)

Tails

ASK SOMEONE ELSE!

N — What are three things that are good to talk about with almost any person your age?

M — Describe a play activity you enjoy doing with other kids at school recess.

L — Describe what you do on Saturdays between dinner time and bedtime.

K — Describe what you do on Saturdays between lunch and dinner time.

J — Describe three interests a grown-up in your home has that are different from your own.

I — If a friend was visiting and the electricity went off in your home, what could you play?

105

THE PLAY AND HANGING OUT ACTIVITY FINDER

Two or more people take turns asking a question or making a suggestion. This can help people to explore fun things they might do together.

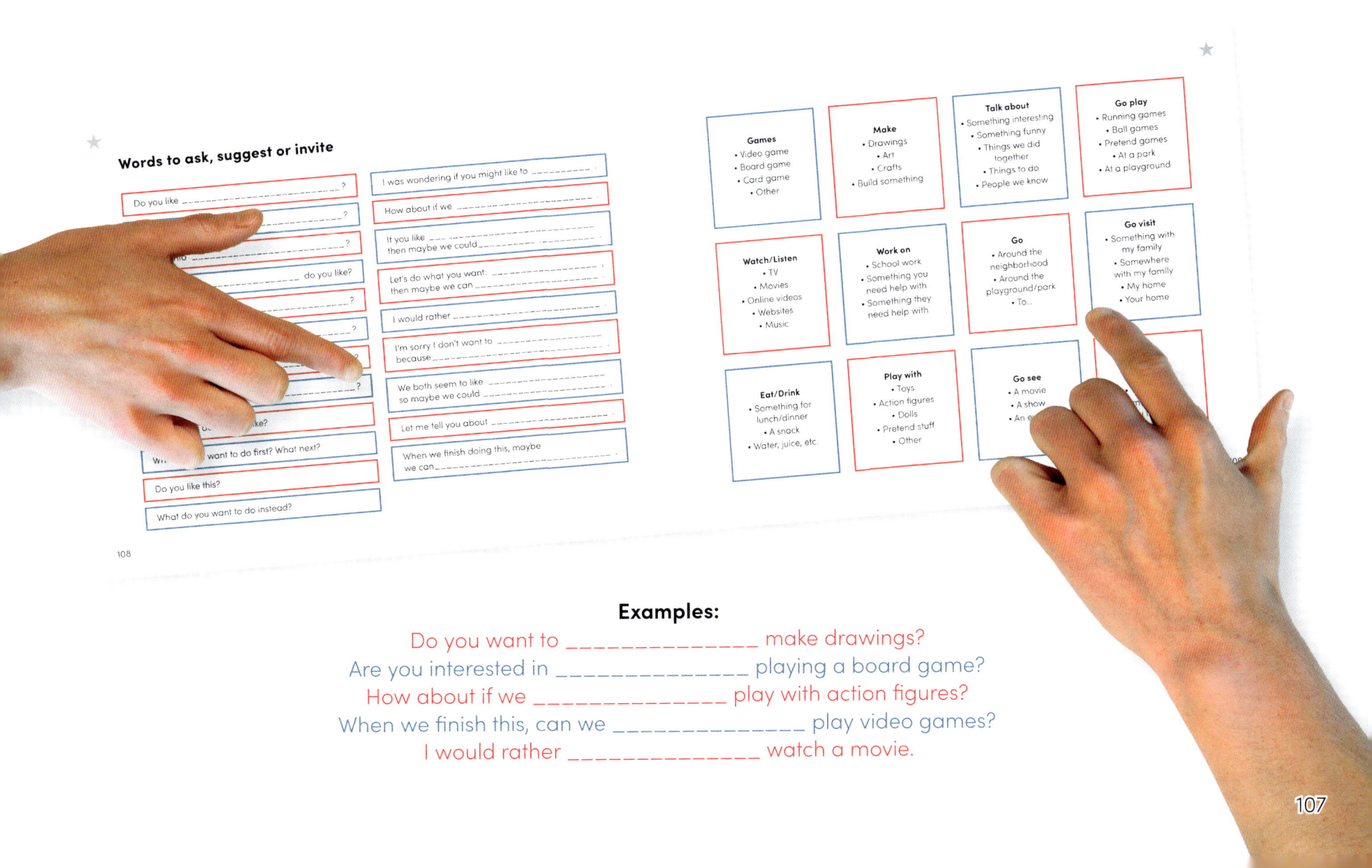

Examples:

Do you want to _____ make drawings?
Are you interested in _____ playing a board game?
How about if we _____ play with action figures?
When we finish this, can we _____ play video games?
I would rather _____ watch a movie.

Words to ask, suggest or invite

Do you like _____?

Do you want to _____?

Are you into _____?

What kind of _____ do you like?

Are you interested in _____?

What is your favorite _____?

Do you feel like _____?

Are you in the mood to _____?

What things do we both like?

What do you want to do first? What next?

Do you like this?

What do you want to do instead?

I was wondering if you might like to _____ .

How about if we _____ .

If you like _____
then maybe we could_____ .

Let's do what you want: _____ ,
then maybe we can _____ .

I would rather _____ .

I'm sorry I don't want to _____
because_____ .

We both seem to like _____
so maybe we could _____ .

Let me tell you about _____ .

When we finish doing this, maybe
we can_____ .

Games	**Make**	**Talk about**	**Go play**
• Video game • Board game • Card game • Other	• Drawings • Art • Crafts • Build something	• Something interesting • Something funny • Things we did together • Things to do • People we know	• Running games • Ball games • Pretend games • At a park • At a playground

Watch/Listen	**Work on**	**Go**	**Go visit**
• TV • Movies • Online videos • Websites • Music	• School work • Something you need help with • Something they need help with	• Around the neighborhood • Around the playground/park • To…	• Something with my family • Somewhere with my family • My home • Your home

Eat/Drink	**Play with**	**Go see**	**Contact**
• Something for lunch/dinner • A snack • Water, juice, etc.	• Toys • Action figures • Dolls • Pretend stuff • Other	• A movie • A show • An event	• My friend: • Your friend: • Someone I want you to meet:

Avoid leaving negative "memory files" in other people's minds

When you play and hang out, you should try hard to avoid putting bad thoughts and feelings in other people's minds.

They might remember these things a long time.

Directions:

Think of a time when things did not go well, and you might have left negative memories in someone's mind.

Write words and draw pictures in each square.

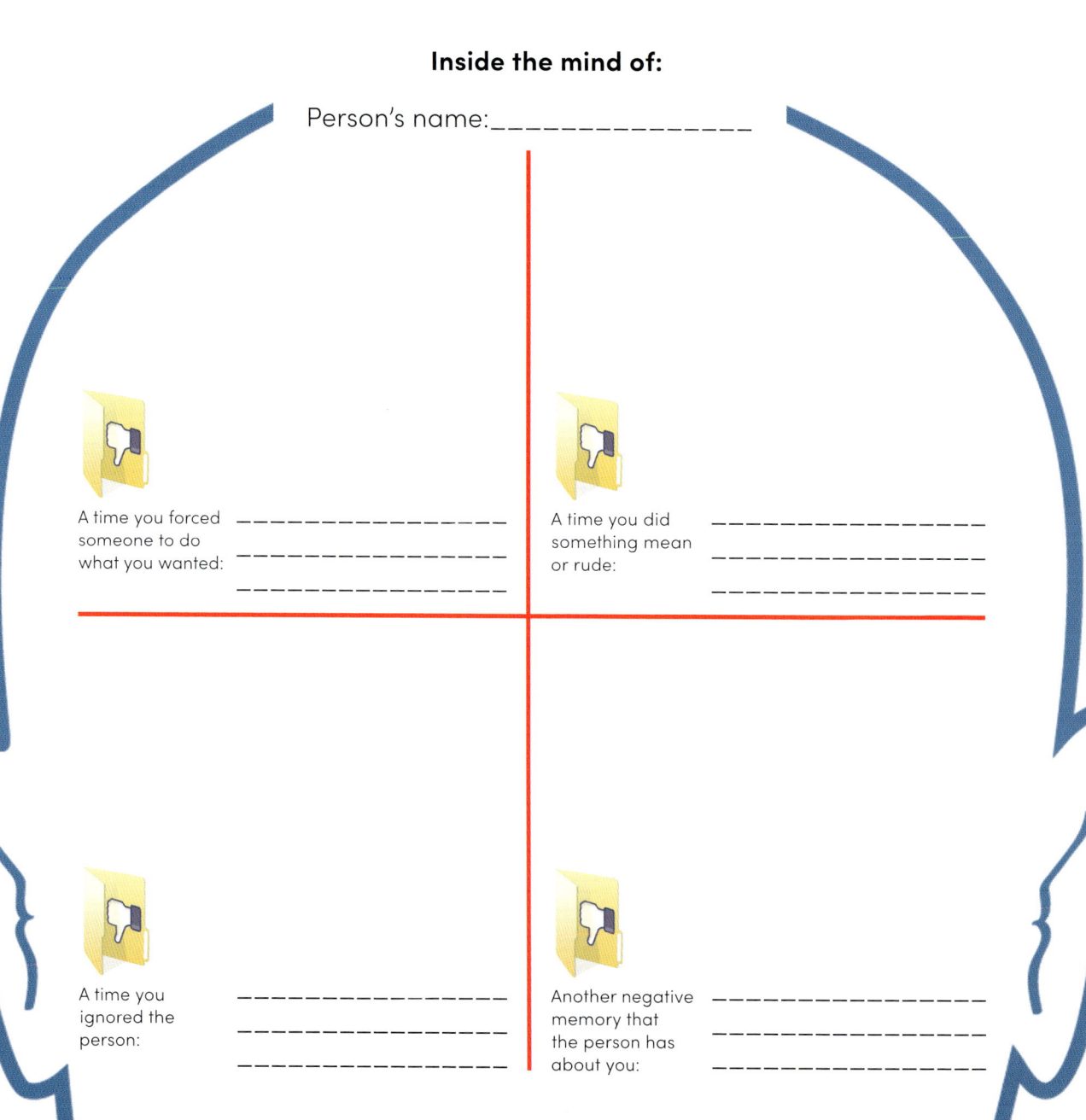

Inside the mind of:

Person's name:_____

A time you forced someone to do what you wanted: _____

A time you did something mean or rude: _____

A time you ignored the person: _____

Another negative memory that the person has about you: _____

Leaving good "memory files" in other people's minds

When you play and hang out with people, it is important to leave good thoughts and feelings about you in their minds.

That way, the person might want to spend more time with you in the future.

Directions:

Think of someone you know that you played with or hung out with.

In each square, write words, and draw small pictures, showing what kinds of good memories you left in the other person's brain.

Inside the mind of:

Person's name:_____

When you played something the other person liked: _____

When you helped the person with something: _____

When you let the other person pick what to do for a while: _____

Another nice memory you left in their mind: _____